T0149724

HOW TO BE
HUMAN

A Story and Path on How to Live with Ease

Annelieke de Vries

BALBOA.
PRESS
A DIVISION OF HAY HOUSE

Balboa Press books may be ordered through booksellers or by contacting:

Balboa Press
A Division of Hay House
1663 Liberty Drive
Bloomington, IN 47403
www.balboapress.com.au
1 (877) 407-4847

Print information available on the last page.

ISBN: 978-1-5043-1197-7 (sc)
ISBN: 978-1-5043-1198-4 (e)

Balboa Press rev. date: 07/20/2018

Contents

Dedication vii

Foreword ix

Introduction xi

1 A girl called Annelieke, and conditioning of the brain 1

2 When trauma happened 13

3 Coping through sex, drugs and therapy 22

4 Conditioning, and generations of trauma 35

5 Living the dream and letting it go 42

6 The journey to self-love 57

7 How drugs changed my world 69

A Final Word 75

References 81

Dedication

This book is dedicated to my beautiful family, friends and all my clients, my therapists and teachers that have supported me in my growth. It is because of all of you that I am where I am today. I am forever grateful for all of your stories filled with wisdom, your uniqueness, and your love and support for me and the work I do. This book would not have been possible without you.

Foreword

I might be human, but I have struggled with this fact. I have always felt different than other people. More sensitive, more emotional. My highs seemed higher than the norm, my lows lower. People did not understand me very well and neither did I understand myself. I was labelled with Anxiety, Depression, and features of Borderline Personality Disorder. Thirty-three years it took for me to undo all the conditioning I endured in this world. It took me all this time to find myself, to remember who I truly was. Thirty-three years I was on a pursuit of happiness, always hoping that the next thing would bring me what I was so desperately craving. I never thought my search for happiness would lead me to where I am today.

Today, I know exactly who I am and what my purpose is in this life. I am, what people like to call, awakened. I am no longer trapped in the waking sleep state that, we are taught to believe is 'true consciousness'. I am no longer trapped in a cycle of material wealth, fear and a pursuit of happiness that might exist somewhere in the future. Today, I am at peace every single day. Even when sadness, fear or anger come into my being, I welcome it with compassion and peace. I no longer live in the world I used to live in. A world full of fear, hate, war and poverty. Today, I live in a world where everything flows, and beauty and abundance are everywhere.

How is that possible? You might ask. That is what I am hoping to explain in this book. My lifelong search for personal growth and fifteen years of experience as a Social Worker, has given me numerous insights into the human experience and the tools to come back to my true self.

We live in a world where most of us have lost the art of sharing. We focus on what is mine, not on what is ours, or what can benefit the whole community. Instead of sharing knowledge and tools, we copyright them, so no one else can reap the benefits. And in my eyes, that's exactly where we went wrong. By cutting our connection to others and the earth, we have cut off a part of who we are. It has send us on a path of ego and individualism.

As the darkness in our world is rising, so is the light. More and more people are awakening and are realising that we are all part of one consciousness, one energy. Even science is starting to catch up and show us 'evidence' of our energetic selves and the connection between all living beings. We are starting to realise that the only way to find true happiness and to get out of this cycle of fear, is to reconnect. We are learning to connect again to ourselves, and this is leading to reconnection to others and the planet we live on.

This is my way of connecting with all of you. By sharing my story and the tools that have helped me, to get where I am today. Because I realise that we are all one. Because I want others to live in the beautiful world I see now every day. A world where everything flows and I co-create and manifest my dreams into reality.

I hope this book will give you the information that you need to remember who you truly are. To come back to a place of happiness, love and compassion for yourself and all beings on this planet. To find the courage to share your story, so others can be inspired and encouraged to brave their fears. To break free from this endless cycle of struggle and suffering, and learn how to live this life with love, ease and purpose.

Introduction

Question everything

I have written this book to help you find your truth. Every human being in this world is unique, and it is our uniqueness that is our strength. It is what makes this world so beautiful. Unfortunately, many of us have grown up to see this as a flaw. We have learned to adjust, so that we fit in with the beliefs that are fed to us about ourselves and the world.

Many of us have grown up to believe there is only one truth and one reality. You might have been raised in a certain religion, that has enforced upon you that this religion is the only true one. Or you have been brought up in a family where you have been taught that certain groups in our society are better than others. My view is that everyone's reality is different, and therefore everyone's truth is different. I am not here to tell you what your truth is. I merely offer you information and tools that I hope will help you discover your own truth, as they did for me and many of my clients.

There is no right or wrong truth, or only one way to see reality. Everyone's reality is equally true and important. Just because you might not understand another person's reality and perceptions, does not mean that your reality is the better or only one. I have encountered many 'awakened' people and 'spiritual leaders' who preached their truth. Because they have awakened and found their connection to self and the universe or God, they think they have figured out the one path that is the only right path. There is not one path. There are many paths that lead to the same thing.

No one can tell you what your path is, as they are not you. You are unique.

There is only one of you, and only you know what feels right for you. Others can tell you their stories of how they got through difficult times, and it might help you. Or it might not. Your intuition, your body knows what feels right. Trust that feeling.

I encourage you to QUESTION EVERYTHING. Never take on anything anyone tells you, without thinking about whether and how this information might fit into your world. Do not take anything in this book on as your truth, just because it is written down. Be critical, reflect upon the new information you are about the receive. Take only that what fits with you and your uniqueness. Only then, will you achieve what has inspired me to write this book in the first place: to rediscover your true self and live a life filled with love, ease, balance and gratitude.

The use of language

One of the things that separates humans around the world, is the use of language. We come from different countries and speak different languages and this makes it hard to connect with each other. But language separates us on more levels than just this one.

We require language in order to make sense of the experiences we have and the world around us. Our senses send us messages to our brain, which then sifts through our memory to establish what sensation we experience, and how we feel about it. We have learned that everything we see, hear, feel, smell or taste, has a name. Depending on the culture and family you were born in, and the experiences you have had with particular sensations, our brain attaches a judgement to the experience and finds words that best describe it.

For example, if I grow up in a culture and family where I receive constant messages that women who are thin are more attractive than women who have more weight, my brain will automatically attach a negative judgement to seeing round curved women. The same goes for skin colour, religion, foods, etc. This is not a conscious process, it happens in a part of the brain that is not aware. And it happens rapidly, within the first couple of seconds we are confronted with a sensation. This process is called unconscious conditioning. Everyone does it. It is not something we can help, but merely a result of conditioning by upbringing, culture and previous experiences.

What I am particularly interested in, is that this happens strongly with language. The words we use, automatically trigger a reaction, either positive or negative. Especially when I talk to people about spirituality or religion, I ensure I use multiple words to explain the same thing. If I only talk about God, I lose all the people that have had bad experiences with an organised religion. So instead, I say: "God, positive energy, the universe, lifeforce, or whatever you feel comfortable calling it".

In my experience, we are all talking about the same energy. We just use different terms to describe them. And you can lose someone's attention easily, if that person gets stuck on the word you use instead of the experience you are trying to describe. Almost everyone believes that there is something that is bigger than ourselves, but it is the words we use that stop people from listening to us. By using multiple words to describe the same thing, I ensure the person understands the experience I am trying to describe, and give them an opportunity to tell me which word they find most appropriate for this experience.

I will use many words in this book you might not be familiar with, or which trigger a strong (unconscious) association or judgement. For this reason, I have added a list in the back of this book to describe some of the psychological and spiritual terms used. Please have a look at it now, so you are familiar with the words used in this book and their meaning to me. I invite you to choose the terms and adjust my language in this book, with words that fits with your reality.

A bit about the information and tools in this book

The information and tools in this book are based on the therapy models and information that have helped me and many of my clients to find our path back to our true selves. I want to acknowledge the work of Dr Russ Harris, Dr Christopher Germer and Dr Janina Fisher as their work has made an exceptional contribution to my healing and the writing of this book. This is not an all-inclusive self-help book. This is my story, linked to the information and other resources that have helped me heal. See it as a map, with just enough information and direction to help you find your own path.

Anything that is new, creates a certain amount of uncomfortability in us. It is our mind and body's way of saying 'Hey, I have not experienced this before'. Often when we try something new, our body perceives it as a threat at first. When I started meditating, my mind and body hated it. My mind kept telling me it would not work for me. Instead of feeling calm and relaxed, my body tensed up. But when I persisted, both mind and body started to get used to this new way of being. It took me about a month before meditation became easier, and before my mind and body stopped protesting so loudly. Remember that change will always bring a certain amount of uncomfortability. This is a sign that you are growing and learning something new. I also ask you to remember that everyone is different and if something really does not feel right, it probably is not right for you.

Some of the information or tools in this book can trigger powerful emotional reactions. People with serious mental or physical health issues are advised to consider these, when going through this book. If you are seeing a therapist, you might want to check with them first prior to implementing some of the tools described. Talking to a friend or a professional can help you release things safely, if you feel overwhelmed.

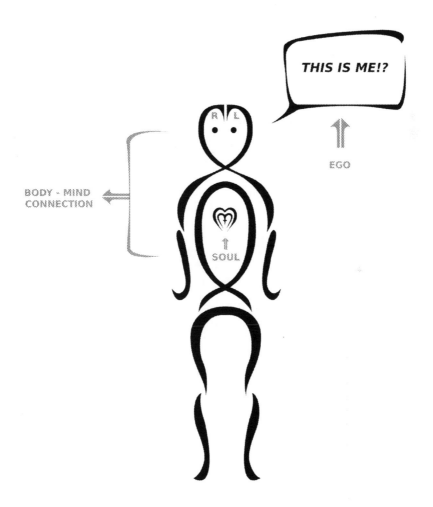

The Human Condition

1

A girl called Annelieke, and conditioning of the brain

I was born on the 20th of February 1984 in Delft, The Netherlands. The middle child, an older brother and younger sister. My parents named me Annelieke de Vries. I was a happy girl growing up in a supportive middle-class family. I was very close to my siblings, had pets I loved very much and friends I saw every day. I was an independent, sensitive, intelligent, creative, social little girl. I was a free spirit, in touch with my soul and the world around me.

Growing up in a western culture was a privilege and a burden. I was lucky to grow up in a country with good health care and education that supported creative thinking, innovation and philosophical discussion. I had access to all I needed, and more. But there was also a downside. One I only realised in the last few years. I was put through the western education system. My brain was trained to think, problem solve and focus on the future. I stopped being in my body. I was encouraged to think and to achieve. Then trauma happened. A few events that shook up my world. The thinking, the worrying, got worse and turned into fear.

The culture I grew up in, is probably the culture you know. A culture that is westernised, that focusses on achievements, money, career, marriage. Our brains conditioned to be in thinking mode. Focussed on the future goals we have set for ourselves by the standards and expectations of our family and culture. I learned to forget who I truly was and had no understanding at all of what this life was about. My true self got lost in systems built on conditioning and fear. The thing was, I did not know I was living in constant fear until only a few years ago. I was living just like everyone else knew.

When I migrated from the Netherlands to Australia, I started working as a counsellor. Many of my clients had a history of trauma. I started learning more about trauma and the human brain. It opened my eyes. This was an important piece of the puzzle I was missing for myself and my work. Understanding the brain and the connection between the mind, body and trauma helped me understand myself and my clients better.

My journey of self-growth and the work with my clients over the last decade, have helped me find the tools that I needed to let go of all that conditioning and fear. To start living with ease, joy and purpose. Understanding how the brain and mind-body connection work, is vital to understanding the human condition. It was the first piece of information that helped me to understand my humanness, and the first thing I want to share with you.

1.1 A bit about the brain

Our brain is made up out of many parts, but I am going to keep things simple. There are many books written by knowledgeable people in this world on this topic, and I encourage you to explore the internet and the library if you want to know more. This is my perception on how I see things, not necessarily how things are in your world. I invite you to research anything you feel you need to in order to find your truth.

We live in a world where get overloaded with information constantly, and we get lost in the details. We end up feeling overwhelmed and unable to filter out the information that is actually important to us. Our brain is made up out of many parts, but I only discuss those parts that I perceive as important for now: the left and right brain half, and the mind-body connection.

The left part of our brain is the part that plans, solves problems, produces thoughts and stores memories in words and pictures. Some call this our thinking brain and it is associated with male energy. It helps us plan and organise our lives and is able to look at the past and future. The left brain also has the ability to cope by 'going on with normal life', no matter what happens. This explains how a woman who gets beaten by her husband, is still able to go to work, be a mother and socialise with friends.

The right part of our brain is the part that is responsible for non-verbal language, body language. It helps you with interpreting emotions, sensations and facial expressions. It is home to our creative energy and is associated with female energy. It is the part where emotional and sensory memories are stored. Trauma is stored as a body response in the right brain. This is also the part from which our instinctive survival responses are activated.

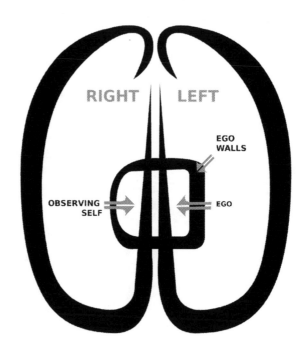

The Brain

The ego and our sense of self

To keep things simple, I am going to say that the left brain is home to the ego. The ego is our personality, our sense of self. It holds our beliefs about who we are, about others and the world we live in. Some people will tell you that having an ego is bad. It is not. We need an ego in order to have a sense of who we are in this life on this planet. Without an ego, we have no sense of self. And without a sense of self, we are not human.

The ego is surrounded by walls. When we talk about someone with a strong ego, we talk about the ego walls. Someone with thick ego walls, has a strong sense of self and strong beliefs about themselves, others and the world they live in. When the walls are too thick, these beliefs and the sense of self become rigid. Walls that are too thick, do not allow new information to penetrate. The persons sense of self does not change, even if they have experiences or new information that allows them to grow.

When our ego walls are too thin, we do not have much of a sense of self. Our beliefs are easily changed by external and internal influences, such as friends, family, media, emotions and pain. Someone who has thin ego walls, feels unsure about who they are and how they fit into this world. They are easy influenced by other people. Their beliefs about themselves, others and the world can change strongly with the events that occur in their lives. This can be very ungrounding. Not having a sense of self means not having a base upon which to stand. It can lead to feelings of depression and anxiety. This is what happened to me, and to the majority of the people I have worked with.

Someone who is balanced, has an ego with walls that are strong enough to keep them grounded, to know who they are in life. To stick to their own beliefs, despite what other people say. But they also have walls that are thin enough to let in new information, so their beliefs and sense of self can change. This enables someone to stay flexible and continue to grow. The ego and ego walls are conditioned by culture, where we live and who we interact with. It can be strengthened or broken down by our life experiences. The ego walls are our protection. They help us stay grounded and help us feel safe when we are undergoing changes, internally or externally.

The soul and the observing self

The right brain is the space that holds a part of us that many refer to as the observing self. It is the part that can just notice, observe everything. It can notice the thoughts produced by the left brain. It can notice the feelings in the body. It is the part that notices the smell, sight, touch and taste of things in detail with complete presence. This is a part of ourselves that just is, a part of us where we are able to be an observer in our own lives. All of us have this observing self. However most of us are used to being in our thinking selves. We are trained to use our thinking brain. That is what gets us through school and work to make the money for the things we want to buy in order for us to be happy. Our observing self has been neglected in the Western culture. Slowly we are starting to remember the importance of training and strengthening this muscle.

The physical, emotional and mental benefits of mindfulness are becoming more widely recognized in the western world. By practising yoga, meditation or other mindfulness exercises, you can strengthen the observing self. This is important, as the observing self is a point from which you can connect directly to your soul and the divine. The soul is what some people call their heart, intuition or their higher self. It is that part of us that is connected to all other living beings on this earth. It is the energy that connects us all. It holds our true identity, our purpose and all the knowledge of the world. Your soul knows what is best for you and when you trust it, your intuition and connection to all energies within and without grow stronger.

Mind-body connection

There is a strong connection between the mind and the body. A constant relay of messages between the mind and the body occurs every second of our life. The senses (touch, taste, smell, sight, sound) feed information to the brain. The brain filters the information and interprets it. It makes a decision and signals the body to respond accordingly.

The right brain is connected with the left body half, the observing self and female energy. When we strengthen the observing self, we can observe our own thoughts and behaviour and connect to our intuition or soul more easily. We can observe how our body responds to situations, people and sensations. The left brain is connected with the right body half, the thinking self and male energy. The left brain can make sense of what our body feels by analysing it. We need the left brain to analyse the messages, sensations and events observed by the right brain in both our inner and outer worlds. The more we observe and reflect on our body responses and thought patterns, the more we learn about ourselves. This helps us understand the messages that our bodies give us.

How we treat our body and how we treat our mind, has an influence on the other. If we choose to eat unhealthy food or not give our body enough nutrients, it will affect our way of thinking. If we chose to surround ourselves by situations or people we do not feel safe with, our body activates the stress response and we cannot think clearly. Our soul constantly gives us signals through our body, messages to help guide us to what is good for us. We just need to know how understand these messages correctly.

1.2 Getting back in touch with our intuition

I believe everyone has all the knowledge and wisdom inside them, to make the decisions that are right for them. It is that feeling you get when you have a hunch, a feeling that something is not right or very right for you. You might know this as your gut feeling, intuition or soul.

Whatever you call that feeling, every human being has it. What is right and wrong is different and unique to each individual. Sometimes, our intuition or 'radar' to steer away from things or people that are not good for us, gets muddled. This happens because of trauma and the culture and systems we live in. We are so conditioned to make decisions that are sensible, with what is perceived 'right and wrong' in our culture, that many of have lost touch with our intuition.

Animals do not make decisions based on peer pressure or culture. Animals are completely guided by their intuition and a stress response when a threat appears. They just know not to eat that toxic plant, or where to look for water. How often do we hear of animals fleeing a certain area, only for a natural disaster to occur a day later killing thousands of people? Just like other animals, our bodies give us valuable clues to what is good and what is not good for us, we just need to learn how to listen and interpret those feelings.

Especially when we have experienced traumatic events in our life, we can misinterpret our body sensations. The reason for this is that traumatic memory is stored as a body response. It creates a chain reaction of physical and emotional changes when there is something (a trigger) reminding your body of the traumatic experience. This can make it difficult to distinguish between intuition, and the stress response activated by triggers of trauma. I will explain more about what trauma is and the effects of trauma in following chapters.

How to ask your body for answers.

So how do we get back in touch with our intuition? The answer is simple: ASK YOUR BODY! This is a simple exercise I was taught in a workshop and has helped me a lot in regaining the trust in my own intuition.

Ask your body exercise:

Stand up, plant your feet firmly into the ground and take three slow deep breaths. (You can do this exercise seated as well if needed.) If you feel comfortable, you can close your eyes to make it easier to tune into your body. Notice what you are feeling in your body right now, any sensations, any pain or tension, any 'buzzing' or vibration.

Now, in your mind or out loud, ask your body to give you an answer for YES and take a minute or so to see if there is a sensation, feeling or movement that happens.

(Some people get a warm feeling in a certain place in their body, others notice tension in a body part or their whole body might move slightly forward, backwards or sideways.)

If you have noticed the feeling, make a mental note of it and move on to the next question.

Now, again in your mind or out loud, ask your body to give you an answer for NO. Again, take a minute or so to notice the change of sensation, feeling or movement in your body, and make a mental note of it. Repeat both questions to double check the sensations are the same.

THIS IS YOUR GUT, YOUR INTUITION GIVING YOU AN ANSWER.

If the responses are very subtle, you can do the exercise again and ask your body to make the response bigger. If the response is too big (for example your body moves that much forward or backwards you almost fall over), you can ask your body to turn the response down a bit. If you receive a different sensation or movement, you might want to do the exercise another two times to ensure you get a consistent answer.

You can use this response to get answers to important questions in your life. My experience is, that this tool works on questions that involve matters of the heart, not matters of ego. Our intuition only wants to guide us on matters that are truly important.

Sometimes, when we are stressed or very emotional, our intuition gets muddled with a stress response that can create similar sensations. To ensure you are listening to your intuition and that you are getting answers that you can trust, you can ask your body the following question first:

- Am I giving answers that are true to my highest good? (the response should be YES). Is there a reason why I would not? (the response should be NO).
- I want to be sick? (NO). I want to be well? (YES)

If you are getting different answers than the ones state above, you are not being guided by your intuition and I strongly recommend that you do not listen to the answers you receive. Instead, you might want to do something calming and relaxing (such as a going for walk, listening to calming music or taking a bath), and then try again. I recommend that everyone uses these 'double check' questions at first, until you feel you know when and how to get accurate information through your body responses.

1.3 The importance of connection

I have always been a very social person, always interested in people's stories and behaviour. That's why I became a counsellor. I grew up in a tightknit family, where connection to self, others and the world were important values. But it is only since I reconnected to myself, that I truly understand how important connection really is.

As a little girl, I loved the buzz of the city. My mother often reminds me that even as a very young girl, I would point to the lights and people in the pubs in town and say: "That is where I want to go mummy". I love connecting with others, especially strangers. I love meeting new people and hearing their stories, as every story tells me more about myself and the world we live in.

Our worlds have become so big, that many of us disconnect. We stop making friends, talking together and supporting the people in our local community. Instead we spend time texting and putting pictures and status updates on Facebook, Twitter or Instagram. We have become isolated and lonely, inundated with so much information we cannot process it. We get overwhelmed by fear and worry and confused with messages that are fed to us through the internet, tv and videogames.

We build up beliefs around the world that are based on feelings of hopelessness and a lack of control. We do not know what information is true, and what is based on lies and deceit. And the only way to gain some control back and not feel overwhelmed by all that information, is to disconnect. The problem is, that many of us chose to disconnect from the thing that has helped us survive and evolve as a species: other humans.

I remember once experimenting with connecting with strangers. I smiled and said hello to everyone I met on the street in my hometown. Some people said hello and smiled back, but most of them looked at me weird, sometimes even scared. It made me sad to see how something as simple as smiling and saying hello, can already put people in a place of fear and suspicion. We have become scared to connect, to tell our true stories. We have become too concerned that we will be judged or perceived as weird, or different. Every person I meet, seems to have the same 'I am different' or 'I am not good enough' story. And yet it appears that we all want the same thing: To live a happy, healthy life filled with love, ease and purpose.

Connection and evolution

Humans have always lived in groups. From the very early times in the caveman era, we needed others to survive. Men hunted, woman gathered and together they ensured there was enough food for the community to survive. There is a reason why we still have the expression 'safety in numbers' today. Can you imagine how hard it would have been to find enough food or keep safe on your own, in a time where sabretooth tigers and mammoths roamed the earth? Just like many animal species, humans evolved to live in groups for safety and protection. There is another thing that evolution made sure of: that we constantly compare ourselves to our fellow human beings. Back in the day, people lived in small communities and it was important that you adhered to the rules to ensure you were not out casted. As mentioned before, it would be difficult to survive on your own, so 'fitting in' and sticking to the rules and social guidelines of the community were vitally important.

Today, our communities are much bigger. The world of technology has ensured that we are not only connected with people in our own town or city but connected to people all over the world. We see supermodels and celebrities on television and the internet, feeding us constant messages about how we should look, act and feel. Our mind is evolved to constantly compare ourselves to ensure we still fit in, but nowadays we have the whole world to compare ourselves with. No wonder so many young men and women have low self-esteem and develop anxiety and depression, just like me.

How disconnected are you?

More and more people are starting to understand how we can use things such as technology, to re-connect instead of dis-connect. In my world, nothing is bad. It is just how you chose to use it. Technology has many uses, but sometimes, it is helpful to make your world a bit smaller. To have a day off from social media, or not to watch the news for a while. To reconnect with people in your local community, maybe even your family members.

I encourage you to have a think about how you are impacted by the vast amount of information that you receive every day. Has it changed your thinking, your self-esteem, your social connections? Do you know your neighbours? Do you spend more time talking to friends via social media then actually meeting up with them in person? Have you been using technology to connect more to yourself and the things and people you love, or has it made you stop connecting all together?

2

When trauma happened

I remember my first traumatic experience as clear as if it happened yesterday. I was seven years old and a happy, sensitive, caring little girl. It was a day like any other, except that day the police knocked on the door. Growing up in a middle-class family who never had dealings with the police before, this made a huge impression on me. The police told my parents, in front of me and my two siblings, that my father's sister had passed away during her travels in Thailand from a mystery illness. The shock and sadness on my parents faces that day, is an image that has never left me. I felt their pain, their grief so deeply. Six weeks later, a cousin died of leukemia, which hugely impacted on our entire family. About a year later my grandmother passed away. All three deaths on my father's side. You can imagine that the grief in our family was overwhelming.

By the time I was eight years old, I had already experienced death three times in less than two years' time. I was staying with my grandparents on their farm by myself, when my grandfather had a heart attack and fell of the stairs. I remember the ambulance was called and I was kept away from the hallway by the neighbour. I escaped the neighbours grip and opened the door. What I saw that day has been burned in my memory forever. Ambulance brothers around my grandfather, electrodes attached to him everywhere. The medics trying to revive him. It was only a couple of seconds before I got pulled away and the door was shut again.

Four deaths in less than two years. My family grief stricken and my parents developed anxiety around the whereabouts of us children, due to my auntie's death overseas. Little did I know how much all of these events impacted on my mental, physical and spiritual wellbeing.

2.1 What is trauma?

I like to describe trauma to my clients in the following way: We all go through events or experiences in our lives that make us feel incredibly scared, fearful for our safety or the safety of our loved ones. We call these events traumatic if they drastically change the way we feel about ourselves, others and the world we live in, and change our behaviour and body responses in order to cope with the experience.

What is traumatic for one person, might not be traumatic at all for another. This is why, after a natural disaster or the death of a loved one, some people are okay and others are not. This can make it even harder for the person that is not okay and just like I experienced myself, this person might question why they are not coping like others are. They start to believe that there is something wrong with them. The level of trauma after an event depends on many things, including our personality, our coping-strategies, our values and beliefs and the level of support we have. What skills and knowledge do we have to make sense of the experience? How does our culture look at the event and our feelings about it? Do we have supportive family members or friends we can talk to, or access to professional help?

EVERYONE EXPERIENCES TRAUMA IN THEIR LIFE

In my eyes, every one of us experiences the effects of trauma. If it is not something that you have been through in this lifetime, it is trauma from a past life, or from your parents or other family members. Just the fact that you have come from generations of ancestors that were conditioned to live in fear is enough to cause the effects of trauma. As trauma is stored as a body response, it can be completely outside of our thinking, conscious self. Take note of any changes in your body as you are going through this book. Is anything triggering any thoughts, visions, body sensations? This could be a sign that your body is responding to a trigger most likely caused by trauma.

Things that cause trauma

To further illustrate what can be traumatic, let me list some of the events that myself, friends and clients have been through that have caused trauma:

- Divorce and relationship breakdowns
- Death, including suicide and homicide, of a friend or family member
- Natural disasters (earthquakes, house fires, floods)
- Experiencing war
- Life-threatening or terminal illness
- Chronic pain
- Migration, unstable accommodation and homelessness
- Physical or sexual assault
- Childhood abuse (psychological, emotional, physical and sexual) and neglect
- Domestic violence
- Bullying
- Physical, mental or intellectual disability
- Growing up with parents who are mentally or physically ill, addicted to drugs or alcohol, or intellectually disabled
- Being treated adversely due to skin colour, sexual preference or religious beliefs

This list contains only some examples of what can cause trauma. There is no set rule for what will and what will not cause a traumatic response, and how severe the response is varies per individual. I invite you to take a moment to reflect on what traumatic events you might have experienced, and how they have changed your beliefs about yourself, others and the world you live in.

Attachment issues

When we experience a traumatic event, our bodies go into a stress response. After the event ends, the body stays in this fight or fight state for a while. We are in shock. We cannot think clearly, might feel nauseous or unable to eat and have difficulty sleeping. The whole event seems unreal, like a bad dream you are waking up from. This is known as an acute stress response. Usually it resolves itself after a few weeks. After trauma, you require support to feel safe again, so your mind and body can relax and turn off the stress response. If you have good support within yourself and around you, your mind and body calm down. You grieve the losses, release the emotions, and integrate what happened. This way, you can let go of the stress and move forward. A lot of people do this, without realising it.

When we experience trauma in our childhood, it changes our attachment. Attachment is the process of bonding between the parent and the child. If the child's needs are met with nurturing and support, it feels safe. When a child cries, it is in a state of stress. When the parent soothes the child every time the stress response gets triggered, the child learns to calm down and feel safe again. Good attachment leads to a sense of safety within yourself. It leads to more resilience and broadens your window of tolerance. When trauma happens and a child does not receive the care and support it needs, it impacts on the child's sense of safety within themselves. The ability to tolerate their emotions, becomes very small. If we are unable to find the safety and support we need within or without yourself, or if even more trauma happens, we can develop Post Traumatic Stress Disorder (PTSD). We stay in a constant state of stress. This can lead to many physical, emotional, psychological and social problems.

2.2 Post-Traumatic Stress Disorder

After my relationship broke down in 2016, I started working with a kinesiologist. The sessions brought memories from my trauma back to the surface. I always knew that seeing my grandfather being revived was traumatic for me, but I did not realise until recently why. Now I know that it was not just his death that was traumatic, but the attempt to revive him. Even at 8 years old, I knew that his soul already left his body. His body was no longer working. I could not understand why people were trying to stop this process. It was only recently I realised how much those four deaths made me disconnect. The moment those ambulance brothers tried to revive my grandfather, was the moment that I decided that there was no God. Up until then, I was raised Christian and believed in God and Jesus. What I can see clearly now, is that it was the disconnection from my spiritual beliefs, that lead to the disconnection from myself. Not only did I disconnect from my beliefs, but from my feelings and body as well. My dark night of the soul started at eight years of age.

I should have been diagnosed with Post Traumatic Stress Disorder (PTSD), but I was not. Soon after my grandpa died, I developed chronic headaches and stopped writing my diary which I did religiously every day. My parents sought advice from a psychologist, who said I could benefit from writing and drawing about it, which my parents helped me to do. It was not enough. I was in a chronic state of stress, leading to physical health issues and severe anxiety. I often had nightmares about my parents dying and developed ways of coping to make myself feel safer. I started doing everything four times, like turning the light switch on and off. I utilised my little sister and parents to regulate my emotions and deal with the intense feelings of panic and overwhelm I often had. I grew up in a state of constant stress, without realising it. I did not understand why I was depressed and anxious. What I did know however, was that there was definitely something wrong with me.

The stress response

Many of us have heard about the fight/flight/freeze response. I like to call it the stress response. When our senses pick up signs of danger, they send signals to our brain to activate our stress response. It is like alarm bells going off in a part of our brain. It is the left brain that stores memories, except for traumatic ones. These are stored as a body response in our right brain This means that the stress response can happen, without our conscious awareness. Before we even realise, our body is in a state of fight and flight. The right brain steers the parasympathetic nervous system, the system that works without our effort. This includes our heart rate, breathing, hormones and release of chemicals in our brain. When the alarm bells ring, the parasympathetic nervous system gets messages to start preparing for danger. It starts releasing chemicals and hormones (including dopamine and adrenaline), that support us to get ready to fight, freeze or flee.

Fight and flight mode

When this stress response is activated, all functions within the body that are not needed in danger are slowed down or shut down completely. All energy is focussed on getting ready to protect yourself and keep yourself safe. The digestive system slows down, the frontal lobe (the part that helps us think, organise, plan) shuts down, the body takes over. Heart rate increases and breathing becomes shallower. Lots of blood is send to the arms and legs, preparing you to run or fight for your safety. It feels like time slows down, sounds become dull, and there is a single focus on safety. This state of fight or flight is also known as hyper-arousal.

Freeze mode

Sometimes we end up in dangerous situations where escape is not possible. Many of my clients with childhood abuse could not run. They were not able to escape the danger, and so the state of hyper-arousal would not work. If fighting or fleeing do not work, our body applies a third coping mechanism: freeze. The danger or pain is too big to handle. Our mind and body disconnect. We go into freeze mode. Some will leave their body completely, watching the abuse from above or entering a different reality that is safe. Others go into a trance state, undergoing the abuse without feeling anything. This state is also known as hypo-arousal.

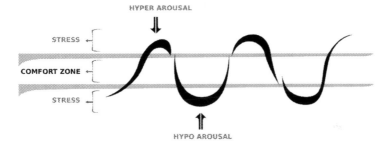

The Stress Response

PTSD diagnosis explained

Post Traumatic Stress Disorder has many symptoms and can display differently in everyone. However, in my experience there are certain symptoms all my clients who have experienced trauma seem to recognise. Men and women seem to cope in different ways, but the symptoms often remain the same.

The most common symptoms are:

- Feeling shame, worthlessness and guilt
- Feeling depressed and irritable
- No longer being interested in things you enjoyed before
- Feelings hopelessness about the future
- Feeling numb, not feeling anything
- Not being able to concentrate
- Difficulty sleeping or sleeping too much
- No motivation
- Feeling overwhelmed
- Not knowing who you are, no sense of self
- Having little or no memories of the trauma
- Flashbacks and/or nightmares about the traumatic event
- Feeling on edge (hypervigilant) all the time
- Difficulty trusting people
- Chronic pain or health issues
- Feeling out of your body or in a constant dream state
- Feeling disconnect to yourself, others and the world
- Suicidal thoughts, sometimes suicide attempts
- Self-harm and risk-taking behaviour
- Abuse of drugs and alcohol
- Disordered eating

When I go through the symptoms of PTSD with my clients, it often triggers a massive response. Their brain is working overtime to integrate the new information, emotions are triggered and their story about themselves and their past is starting to change. It is what happened to me. It was a vital piece of information I needed, to finally understand why I was behaving the way I was.

When there is chronic trauma or multiple traumatic events in someone's life, people develop even more complex thinking and coping patterns. It is a state of chronic PTSD I like to call Complex Post Traumatic Stress Disorder. It has lead them to not only have PTSD, but also continue to attract traumatic events towards them because of the coping mechanisms they developed. It is a vicious cycle of darkness, of undergoing trauma and getting back up, by coping in a way that attracts more trauma.

Many people do not recognise that they have experienced trauma. I only recognised and accepted it within myself two years ago. But they do know they feel different. Depression and Anxiety are common diagnosis for people with trauma. Other clients I have worked with, have been misdiagnosed with Bipolar disorder or Borderline Personality Disorder. Because trauma has so many effects similar to the 'disorders' mentioned above, and because many of us are unaware of our trauma, misdiagnosis is very common. I see it over and over again in my work. Most of my clients are relieved to get the diagnosis of PTSD. It feels right, and it takes away some of the guilt and shame for them. It gives them understanding of why they feel the way they do, and they are able to see it is not their fault.

Some people have large amounts of memories flooding back when they start learning about trauma. This is why it is important to seek professional help if you feel overwhelmed, or all of a sudden start developing physical issues. Remember, trauma is stored as a body response, which often includes pain. You can ground yourself when you are feeling overwhelmed, by doing some simple exercises. More on this in chapter three.

3

Coping through sex,
drugs and therapy

Around fifteen years of age, I plunged into a deep depression and started disassociating. I do not know what was worse. The intense feelings of hyperarousal, or the numbness of not feeling anything. I started self-harming to feel something, to get back into my body. I did not tell my family members. I did not want to burden them with how I was feeling.

The shame was the hardest. I could not understand why I was depressed and did not care whether I lived or died. I was raised in a close, supportive and nurturing middle-class family. I was not abused or neglected, did not grow up in war or domestic violence. I had no reason to feel the way I did, which made the depression even worse. At my lowest point, I was self-harming on a regular basis. I started smoking weed and limited my food intake, as a way of controlling my emotions. When I finally decided to reach out for help, it was my friend and drum teacher who I went to. He was there for me. He helped me stop self-harming, and he became my first boyfriend. It was then that I learned to feel safe within myself by connecting with men.

During my puberty, I had equipped myself with some survival techniques that literally stopped me from killing myself. Men, smoking weed and disordered eating became my coping strategies. Ways to regulate my emotions and feel safe. I was what you could call a 'functioning mental health patient'. Someone that excelled in school, did as she was asked, had lots of friends and seemed like a happy teenager. The difference being that I was not. I was very good at hiding my true feelings and deep dark thoughts from many.

I started smoking weed daily. I started partying, using MDMA and alcohol every weekend. I slept with many men, to find some sense of safety and self-worth. Of course, it only made me feel worse about myself. This made me feel even more unsafe, and so the cravings for sex and drugs would increase. It was a vicious cycle of dependency on men and substances, further increasing my feelings of shame and worthlessness.

Luckily, I also had built up some helpful coping strategies. When I would not feel too bad, I would socialise with my friends, dance at festivals, write my diary and do my art. All these things helped me built myself back up when another man had dumped me, or I felt too dark inside. Even the drugs and partying had its good side. Marihuana helped me to not feel so much and get into my creative energy (my right brain). MDMA helped me to feel the love, to get lost in the moment for a change, and release all I was feeling through dance.

3.1 Coping mechanisms

During our childhood and teenage years, we learn to build certain skills, ways in which we cope. Depending on the culture, family and circumstances we grow up in, we learn how to deal with emotions, thoughts, other people and our environment in a specific way. A way that helps us survive and feel safe. These skills are also known as coping mechanisms.

There are many different ways people cope with things that happen inside or outside of themselves. All of us have both helpful and not so helpful ways of coping. Healthy coping mechanisms are things such as writing a journal, exercise, talking to someone, dancing it out, painting or writing music, etc. Not so helpful or even destructive ways of coping can include getting into fights, abusing drugs, alcohol or people, self-harming to numb the pain, pretending we are fine and putting a mask on. What might be an unhelpful coping mechanism now, has not always been unhelpful. These ways have kept you safe at some stage in your life, just like they did for me. So instead of beating yourself up for the way you cope, be kind to yourself. Recognise that they have kept you protected in the past and helped to keep yourself safe. And the safer you feel within yourself, the more you are able to let go of those ways of coping that no longer serve you.

Recognising your triggers

Triggers are things in your external environment that generate a signal to your brain that something is up. The trigger can be anything from a smell or a sound, a person, event or location, a touch from someone. The body remembers previous traumatic or negative events and starts up the stress response. Before you realise it, you are in a state of fight, flight or freeze. Learning to observe the signals of the stress response in your body and reflecting on what triggered it, is vital to changing this response. The more we understand and recognise our triggers, the easier it becomes to intervene.

If you have a lot of trauma, you can have a lot of triggers. This means that people with complex trauma, can get triggered every hour of the day. It results in a constant state of stress. All of this happens subconsciously and triggers can be very subtle. Because of this, you do not always realise how often you get triggered, and how often this leads to hyper- or hypo-arousal. We cannot take triggers away. There will always be moments where you will get triggered. But by understanding them and learning how to calm your body and mind, you can stop the stress response and refocus your attention on the present moment. In the end, this will mean that you no longer have to avoid people or situations, as we have learned to remain calm and feel safe, no matter what.

I invite you to reflect on your triggers. Are there situations or people you avoid, because they remind you of a bad past experience? Start to get to know your triggers and observe what happens in your body. The aim is not to avoid triggers, but to learn to respond to them differently. However, if you realise that you experience a lot of triggers, it might be worth seeing which triggers you can avoid for now, so you can give you mind and body more rest.

3.2 How painting and partying helped me heal

I feel very grateful to have grown up in a family, where expressive arts were highly appreciated and encouraged. I learned to play the flute, piano and later the drums. I had gymnastic and ballet lessons and did arts and crafts from a young age. I realise now how important those things were for my wellbeing. At least I had built up some constructive coping mechanisms, that later stopped me from ending up in an even darker hole. I would go to techno raves and let myself go through dance. I would paint my feelings on a canvas and then paint the canvas white again, because I did not feel my art was worth keeping. But at least it helped. I was able to express and let go of some of my sadness, stress and pain. But it never took long for the depression and anxiety to resurface.

My love for the arts made me follow my brother's path of studying Graphic Design, to then make the step to Art Academy. I loved drawing and art history, but hated the computer side of my design studies. I spend more time hanging out with my brother in his class, or in the coffee shop smoking weed. It was this year I started smoking all day, every day. I was in a permanent state of disassociation, living in my own little bubble. Most of my time was spend on worrying about the past or the future. The only times I felt present, was when I was playing the drums or when I was dancing or painting. After I decided to ditch Graphic Design and study Social Work, I started feeling more present. My mood improved when I sought psychological support. I knew I needed to work on myself if I was to help other people. The university I went to was big on the arts, and I learned how to use drama, visual arts, dance, storytelling and photography in therapy. It inspired me and helped me heal and transform further.

Expressive arts as a way of healing trauma

When I started studying the brain and the neurobiology of trauma, I realised how much of what I already did naturally was helping me heal my trauma. Through expressive arts (such as dance, visual arts, making music or singing and drama), I was able to access my right brain directly. The arts bypassed my left brain, the part that produces thought and holds memory, including my ego. I learned to use the senses to access and express what was stored in my right brain, in my subconscious mind. And this included trauma.

I have always loved electronic music and danced how my body wants to dance. It makes me feel present and free. When I would dance for long enough on the repetitive beats of electronic music, I would enter a trance like state. Complete presence and bliss. My dancing was based on what is known as bilateral movement. Using, training and connecting both brain halves, by doing repetitive and synchronised movements with both body halves. Bilateral movement includes things like drumming, certain dance styles, cycling, boxing, tai chi, many yoga poses, drawing with both hands, and swimming. I noticed I was doing this process naturally, to help express and heal my emotions and trauma. I loved the idea of strengthening the mind-body connection by doing more bilateral movement. I started sun salutations, painted more, bought a drum and started doing drawings with both hands at the same time. It helped.

The expressive arts are highly undervalued in the world we live in. Many art therapies are not accessible in most countries, and yet this is what is healing people. We can do these arts by ourselves to help heal. Maybe you are already doing a lot of therapeutic work without even realising it?! And if not, I encourage you to have a think about how (and which) expressive arts and bilateral movement could benefit you to heal what is stored in your subconscious mind. And why not just give it a go? Write a poem, draw, dance. It does not matter what the end result is, it is the process of creation that is so healing and transformational.

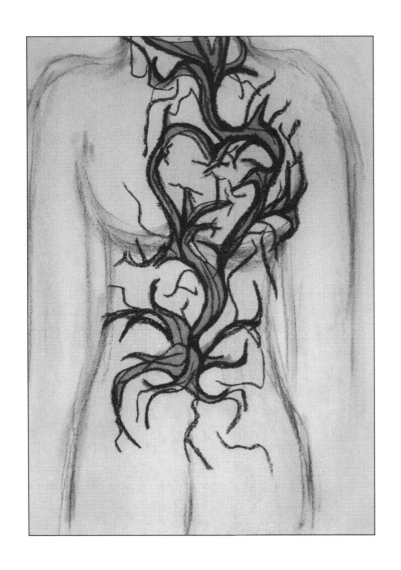

Healing my trauma through art

3.3 The importance of grounding

I learned about the importance of grounding when I studied, and it often came up in workshops that followed after my graduation. I knew a couple of grounding techniques I used with my clients in the mental health inpatient unit, but that was about it. When I started working as a counsellor, I started understanding how to use grounding tools more and more. The more I learned about trauma, the more I understood the importance of helping people get back in their body and connected to the physical world.

I never realised how much grounding would help me. I never thought I needed it. It was not until I started working with clients with complex trauma, that I saw how much I had been disconnected from my body myself. After my relationship broke up, there were a couple of times in that first year where I severely disassociated for a few days. A full disconnection from my body and the world. Isolating myself, feeling like the world was a day dream, and not feeling anything at all. Urges of cutting myself, to get back into my body. I had not disassociated like that since I was a teenager. This time however, I had learned more about grounding and was able to apply my newly learned skills. I was able come back to a place of connection to myself and the world around me.

Nowadays, I do a lot of grounding exercises. I do not often disassociate anymore, but I still think too much. I spend too much time in my mind, left or right brain. It is hard to keep the balance between mind and body, between just observing, just being and thinking. Grounding skills are vital for my own and the mental health of many of my clients, to be able keep the balance right. To come back to being present, to not think, but feel our ways through life.

Ways to ground yourself

I have listed some of the grounding skills that have helped me and many of my clients. I encourage you to reflect on how grounded you are and try out some of the grounding tools below. Notice how you feel in your mind and body. Notice any changes in your thoughts. Many of these tools are useful when you are feeling disconnected from yourself or the world and can be used in any situation. Practising grounding on a daily basis is a good way of building these skills. It helps strengthen the connection to the present, your body and the earth, and helps you remember to ground yourself when you are in a state of crisis.

Some helpful grounding tools are:

- Change your body temperature by splashing hot or cold water on your face and wrists.
  This helps shock the body and temporarily cuts the stress response in the body, giving you an opportunity to do further grounding.
- Take deep, slow breaths from your belly.
  Deep breathing slows down your heart rate and calms the nervous system.
- Push your feet into the ground, feel where your feet are touching the floor or ground.
- Visualise roots growing out of your feet deep into the earth, and roots growing from deep inside the earth to you. Visualise both roots connecting, holding you firmly.
- Lay face down with your belly on the ground and connect to the earth. Breathe deeply through your belly and visualise connecting with the core or womb of the earth, the planet you live on.

3.4 Healing through play

The great thing about my outgoing, clubbing lifestyle, was that I met heaps of new people. One of them was, and still is, particularly important to me: a beautiful woman 9 years younger than me, from Czech Republic. We met on my birthday not long after I broke up with my partner. I posted an ad on Facebook to see if I could get a lift to a party in the Byron hinterland. I received a text offering a pick up from a girl I never met before. I did not know her, and yet this woman went out of her way to pick me up and drive us to this party. We got along straight away.

Not long after we met, she broke up with her boyfriend. I needed a flatmate, and she moved in with me the same week. She has been my best friend ever since. Her caring, nurturing, outgoing and down-to-earth personality were exactly what I needed in a time where I was drowning in pain and loneliness. She cooked and cleaned, she stroked my hair and laid next to me when I was too upset to talk. She shared my interest for electronic music and soon we became 'doof buddies'. Whenever there was a doof (the Aussie version of an outdoor rave), we were there dancing the night away. Her easy going 'I don't care and will try anything' attitude, opened my world up to new situations and experiences. I loved it. She reminded me of my sister, who had always been my best friend, and whom I missed terribly since I migrated.

What I have learned most of all from our friendship, is to not take life so seriously all the time. How important it is to play and have fun. Over the years, I had lost the art of playing. I started to realise how absorbed I was on working on myself and how much my work with depressed, abused and suicidal clients had stopped me remembering the importance of play and having fun. She helped me to have fun again. I had to re-learn to play, to laugh and be silly, to not care but just be and do. It helped me come back to my playful, fun-loving, outgoing true self, which made me realise how healing fun and play truly are. That you do not always have to go into the deep dark corners of our mind and cry, but that you can also heal through fun and joy.

Play more!

I do not play enough. I had to learn how to be a child again, as most of us do. When we get older in life, many of us lose our ability to play. Our western cultures do not encourage play much, once we have become adults. I have wondered whether this is why a lot of people end up having children. Maybe because they can allow themselves to play again.

Being creative and being playful helps us let go of our ego and thinking brain. It helps us feel free, to be like a child again. We are in our right brain, our creative energy when we play. Laughter is equally healing for us human beings. Play and fun in our lives help us heal and nurture our inner child. It helps us forget about all the hard and mundane stuff in life and allows us to let go and enter the dreamtime of our imagination. It calms the brain and strengthens the observing self. It unlocks our creative energy and help us let go and re-energise.

I ask you to reflect on how much play-time you have allowed yourself lately. When is the last time you had a pillow fight, or made a cubby house? Or made silly faces with your siblings, like you used to during dinnertime? I invite you to make time to play every day!

3.5 The journey of getting help

I have always been a keen and easy learner and loved school. I enjoyed gaining new knowledge, presenting to the other kids in my class, writing essays, even doing tests. Primary school was easy for me. Too easy. I was always the first to finish my work and got bored, so the teacher gave me extra work to do. I remember the day I got tested, to see if I was 'specially gifted'. I was not, although my IQ was higher than average. This was the first time I got tested, to see if I was 'normal'. I can see now that this is where the story I made about myself started. The story that I was different, which later turned into the story that there was something wrong with me. It was not until my teens when I saw my first psychologist, that I experienced the impact assessment and diagnosis had on my sense of self.

The process of seeking help was a massive undertaking. To acknowledge I needed help was one thing, to actually make the step and ask for help was another. I was working in mental health and now needed treatment for my own mental health. The shame, stigma and courage I had to brave to access treatment was a massive hurdle. Talking to the doctor, convincing him I really needed help, then being put on a waitlist for months. It was all very discouraging. But I persevered and 3 months after seeing the doctor, I had my first appointment at the mental health outpatient clinic in my hometown.

I remember making sure no one saw me walk into that building. I was worried what people would think if they found out. Luckily my parents were very supportive, which got me over the line to actually get to that first appointment. A long intake assessment followed. So many questions about my life, lots I did not have an answer for. It made me feel even worse about myself. Then lots of assessments to try and diagnose me and make a treatment plan. I was worried. Would I have Bipolar just like my grandmother? Will they put me on medication? A part of me wanted to know what was wrong with me, another part was terrified to know the outcome.

After a full day of assessments and waiting with lots of anxiety for a couple of weeks, I had my second appointment, where I received the report with diagnosis and treatment recommendations. It was all there on paper, in black and white. I remember to this day very clearly what was stated: no Bipolar disorder, anxiety and depression and traits of Borderline and Narcissistic Personality Disorder. Ouch. It was like someone just punched me hard in the face. Pushed in a corner. Labelled. Stamped. So many emotions all at once.

Anxiety and Depression, I could resonate with that. To get labelled traits of personality disorders, that was a different ball game. I worked in the acute inpatient mental health unit. I knew what Borderline and Narcissistic Personality Disorder were. I also knew that (back then), the research stated that personality disorders could not be treated, only managed. I saw how we interacted with and treated patients with personality disorders. And it was not the most supportive and humane treatment. It further damaged my self-esteem and confirmed the story that there was something wrong with me.

Over the next ten years I became the diagnosis. I became Anxiety and Depression. It was a subconscious excuse for me to justify my behaviour and to avoid things that I was uncomfortable with, such as driving in the city or being alone at night. I remember I started warning new friends or potential partners about my mental health. "Just so you know, I am very sensitive and emotional. I go up and down in my mood a lot and I have been depressed when I was 15."

But there was also another side to receiving a diagnosis. At least I could understand some of my behaviour and could give it a name. It made me realise that I was not the only one who felt this way, which made me feel slightly better. I believe now, that if I would have received the right diagnosis of PTSD back then, that it would have been more of a relief then a burden for me. PTSD acknowledges the trauma, where Anxiety and Depression were put down to my family's genepool (my mum had a burn out, my grandmother Bipolar). It would have given me an answer for my addictive behaviour, my highs (hyperarousal) and lows (hypo-arousal), my nightmares and flashbacks, my disordered eating.

Therapy was good for me. I saw my psychologist for 1.5 years every 1-2 weeks for Cognitive Behaviour Therapy, which (back then) was the treatment model that was proven to work the most effectively for my diagnosis. I learned new ways of thinking and new ways of coping. I started writing a journal and started painting how I felt, which helped me a lot. I count myself lucky that I have always found the right therapist for me straight away. I never had to go through that horrendous process of seeing multiple counsellors before you find the one that you feel that click with. I went back to see a psychologist again in my last year of studies and again when my relationship broke down 2 years ago. And I will go again in a heartbeat if I feel I need to. I no longer worry about stigma and understand that it is a strength to be able to acknowledge you need help and ask for it.

Tips for getting the right help

I always advise anyone to find the therapy and therapist that fit with you. I have found the best therapists to work with through word of mouth, so it is worth asking around! Everyone is unique and so you need to look for what fits best for you. If you chose to go see someone and you do not feel a click, it is okay to find someone else. Find someone you feel at ease with after the first meeting. Therapy is based on the relationship build between client and therapist, so it is vital that the connection is good. If you have (had) a bad experience with therapy, do not give up! There are many skilled and not so skilled therapists out there, so find the right one. Friends, family, your doctor or other services might know someone they would recommend in your local area.

The type of therapy is again an individual choice. Your doctor or family members might recommend counselling, where you feel it is best to see a kinesiologist or do dance therapy. Choose whatever feels right for you, not what others want you to do. Working on trauma for most people will include a range of therapies at different times in their healing journey, just like I did. You might decide that you do not need any therapy at present. That your creative outlets, your dancing or meditation is the only healing you require.

Many countries work with a system of requiring assessment and referral from your doctor, to access free or rebated mental health services. With the technology we have today, there are many free and paid online services, including counselling support. Try and find a trusted mental health organisation and look up reviews before you commit to anything. The benefit of phone and online support is that you can stay anonymous. Most Western countries have 24-hour helplines for specific support, such as carer support, mental health, domestic violence or drugs and alcohol.

4

Conditioning, and generations of trauma

I always knew that mental illness could be passed on through our DNA. Genetic sensitivities are common knowledge, some families suffer more from certain illnesses than others. I received my phobia for spiders from my mother. I vividly remembering her screaming and jumping up and down on the bed because of a spider in the room. What I only realised later in life, is how much of my parents' anxiety and emotional patterns were passed on to me. My mum and dad became very anxious about our kids' safety and whereabouts, after my auntie had passed away overseas. My mother's burn out during my teens had contributed significantly to the deterioration in my own mental health. My father's consumption of alcohol (even if it was only two glasses every night), contributed to the development of my dependence on substances as a way of coping.

How much of this anxiety was passed on, became evident when I migrated to Australia to be with my partner at the time. I remember he did not understand why I always wanted to know what time he would be home. He could not understand my state of terror if he was not home at the time he said he would. He did not realise I already envisioned him dead on the side of the road or drowned in the ocean.

I also got passed on many gifts from my parents. The way they raised me and my siblings, was one where emotional expression, deep discussion and expressive arts were encouraged. My parents allowed us to be who we wanted to be. I grew up with strong values. To have respect for all living beings and to never judge anyone by their cover. I am forever grateful to my parents for the openminded empathic attitude I build in my childhood.

4.1 Intergenerational trauma

We inherit many things from our parents, including their DNA and their unresolved trauma's. Their life experiences and trauma impacts directly on how they parent us. They might be more anxious, or cope by abusing others or substances. The more trauma the parents have endured, the bigger the impact on their children. This is why we see cycles of abuse happen over and over again in families. The trauma and the coping mechanisms are literally handed over from one generation to the next. Sometimes for so long, that the abuse is encoded on the deepest level of our being: our DNA. The trauma is stored as a body response and when trauma happens for long enough, it changes us on this bodily level. Trauma becomes embedded in every cell in our being. When trauma is handed over from one generation to the next, it is known as intergenerational trauma.

Examples of intergenerational trauma can be seen in the Indigenous cultures all around the world, including Australia. The shame, guilt and losses from the first Aboriginal people that were hunted like animals, babies stolen from their families, separated and abused, is still impacting on the Aboriginal families and children born today. I witnessed intergenerational trauma for the first time in Germany. I was fifteen years old and on a student exchange week. I saw and felt the young people's shame of being German, ashamed of their history, more than 40 years after the end of the Second World War.

Trauma can be so deeply embedded in our countries culture and history, that we are used to it. We do not always see the symptoms ourselves. Sometimes, it takes an outsider to bring it to the light and make us reflect upon our own culture's history. Have you ever thought about how intergenerational trauma fits in your family and culture's history?

4.2 What's in a culture?

I did not realise how lucky I was to grow up in The Netherlands, until I migrated to Australia in 2007. The first year in Australia was difficult for me. I did not know anyone except my partner, leaving everything behind. My family, my friends, my language, my permanent job. I decided to risk it all for love. I am glad I did.

Living in The Netherlands was difficult for me. I was used to limited space and lots of people, but the weather was something I never got used to. It can be grey and rainy for weeks on end, without one ray of sunshine. Every winter I became depressed. The lack of sunshine and the feeling of being trapped inside, were detrimental for my mood. Yet I never ever contemplated living in another country. I loved The Netherlands for many reasons. The openminded, diverse and innovative culture in which I grew up, had a huge impact on my thinking. Debates and deep discussion were a common occurrence amongst family and friends. Cultural and creative activities were part of my daily life. When I migrated to Australia, I soon realised that this was not the norm everywhere.

People expected me to integrate easy. I was white, from a Western country with a similar culture and spoke the English language well. But it was everything but easy. I was grieving so many losses. My family and friends of course, but also the loss of language and my culture. I found it difficult to fit in and express myself in a second language, especially emotionally. I often lacked the words in English to express how I felt. Miscommunication between me and my partner was a common occurrence that first year.

When I got my first job as a counsellor in Sydney, I struggled. I had done my studies in Dutch and excelled in expressing myself verbally and in the written word. Now I had to start from scratch. I found it hard to understand some clients, due to their accent and the slang used in the Aussie culture. The longer I lived in Australia, the more I adjusted. My English got better and I was able to express myself better in my personal and work life. I started to understand the culture and the challenges of white and indigenous Australians better. And I loved the active outdoor lifestyle and the vast amount of space and nature in this country. Slowly I started to become more Australian.

With this process of integration, I also started to lose my connection to the Dutch culture. I grasped onto my own heritage in a way I had seen with my Turkish and Moroccan friends back home but had never understood. The things I used to hate back home, I now adored and welcomed into my life. Delft blue pottery, Dutch food, the Dutch flag, the Dutch public holidays. It all became important for me. I almost felt patriotic, which is something I had never been in my life. I started romanticizing my home country and culture and held on to Dutch traditions more strongly than I had ever done, because I felt I was losing a part of me.

Culture and the belief system

Our way of thinking and being is influenced my many things. The way you are parented, the school you go to, the friends you have, all impact on our sense of self, others and the world around us. The culture we grow up in, hugely impacts on the subconscious conditioning we endure in our lives. It shapes our way of thinking, our values, our goals and actions.

Every country and culture has its own specific cultural beliefs and history. We can see the huge difference in values between Western and African or Asian countries, but we often do not recognise the subtler differences between cultural beliefs that makes each country unique. By visiting or living in different countries, we open ourselves up to new experiences and cultural beliefs and values. It helps us see things from a different perspective, breaking our ego walls to refresh the way we look at our own culture and beliefs.

Travel more, grow more

Have you travelled or lived in a different country? Or is this something you are contemplating? Travelling and submerging myself in a different culture, has been one of the fastest and easiest ways for me to grow within myself. You are forced to reflect upon yourself and your beliefs. You have to let go of expectations and perceptions as you encounter the opposites.

Even if travel is not an option, it is not hard to immerse ourselves in a different culture these days. With open eyes, respect and curiosity, there are always opportunities to expand our horizon Visit a local mosque or Chinatown. Connect with someone you would not normally connect with. Take Salsa classes. Experiencing other cultures opens our eyes. It helps us reflect upon our own cultural habits and beliefs.

4.3 How my job made me sick

I was eighteen when I started working in the mental health hospital. It did not take long before I started working on the closed acute inpatient unit. I loved everything about it. I loved helping people. But I also loved the intensity, the danger of psychotic and aggressive clients, having to restrain and heavily medicate people, only to help them stabilise and see them get back to their normal selves. I know now that I loved these dangerous work environments because of my PTSD.

I was so used to be in a state of hyperarousal, of fight and flight, that it felt safe for me to work in an environment that triggered this response. Hyperarousal had become my 'safe zone', relaxation a state that was unfamiliar to me. What I was not aware of, was that work was further traumatising me. Assaults on staff and suicide attempts by clients were a common occurrence in the unit I worked, and this was something that we 'just had to deal with'. It was part of my work and unfortunately there was not much support or understanding for the extreme circumstances me and my colleagues worked in. It became 'normal' and something I took as just another part of my work in the mental health unit.

It was making me sick. The constant state of fight and flight was leaving me exhausted. When I moved to Australia and started working as a counsellor, some of this exhaustion left. I no longer needed to be on edge all the time. I learned to be okay with a state of calm at work, although a part of me still craved the high intensity of the inpatient work. I focussed on working with the most complex clients to find the intensity again. The clients with complex and long histories of trauma.

After six years of working in the local public health system as a casual, I was finally successful in obtaining a permanent position. This was something I had wanted for years. Like most of us, I thought the permanent job would give me what I wanted: safety and security, the ability to get another mortgage to get stability in my living situation. The effect was the opposite. It made more exhausted and drained.

I hated the separation between those with and those without money, the hierarchy and vast amounts of paperwork in the public health system. I never felt I had enough time to do my work properly. It left me exhausted and unsatisfied after each day of work. The only thing that kept me going was my clients. But I was not able to be there fully for my clients. I was plagued by migraines and chronic pain as a result of constant stress. Three months into my permanent role, I made the decision to quit. To focus solely on my private practice, which I had slowly started to build over the last 6 months. Many people told me not to do it, that permanent jobs are hard to come by and I should praise myself lucky to have one. I did it anyway. It was the second most self-compassionate thing I had ever done for myself.

The effects of our jobs on our wellbeing

Our values are important. They are our compass in life, steering us into the direction that is best for us. When we work in a system that does not support our values, it impacts on our whole being. It becomes harder to enjoy what you do. Every work environment has its own work culture. Just like the culture of the country we grow up in, the work culture impacts on our sense of self. If we work in a place where we are accepted and respected for who we are and what we do, we feed of that positive energy. If the workplace is a place of struggle and competition, it will drain our energy. This can lead to burn-out, depression, anxiety and physical health issues.

For me, it was the best choice to work for myself. To get away from the systems as much as possible. Everyone is different. Some people are able to work in a system that does not support their values, without letting it get to them. They find a way to work with the system. Whatever you chose, the most important is that you feel passionate about what you do and where you work.

You are the only one to know what is the right work place for you. Have a think about how much your workplace supports your wellbeing. Are their values in line with yours? Do you feel energised after work, or drained and exhausted? Does your workplace value self-care as much as you do? Do they look after you and support you in self-development? And most of all, are you actually doing the work you love and dream of doing?

5

Living the dream and letting it go

I had never seen myself do what most people do in this life: buy a pet, get married and buy a house. I just never felt that a 'normal' life was for me. Until I met the man of my life. Or so I thought. He definitely was for almost nine years, and I will be forever grateful for our relationship. His stable, down-to-earth, easy going, caring personality helped me to understand the Aussie culture. He got me to a place where I could feel safe and emotionally stable within myself.

My partner loved going outdoors, especially those places where there is no trace of civilisation. I loved going back to the absolute basics, no phone, no toilets, no showers. Just me, my partner and nature. Having lived in The Netherlands, where there are so many people on such a small piece of (man-made) land, I did not know what it meant to experience the peace and quiet and the overwhelming beauty of nature. I had lost my connection to nature, purely because of where I grew up. My partner helped me reconnect with nature and therefor with a piece of myself, which I had not connected with since my childhood.

Our relationship was beautiful and full of growth for the first six years. We lived in Sydney, then in The Netherlands and New Zealand, before settling down in Byron Bay on the NSW North Coast in Australia. My partner had always wanted to buy a house that he could renovate and could make his home. He was keen to settle down. By this time, I was getting steady work in the local public health service and he build up his own business as an electrician. We got pets, two bunnies, to help me deal with my feelings of grief and loneliness that would still pop up regularly around my migration. We were ready to settle down.

At least, that is what I thought I wanted. I thought I would be with my partner for the rest of my life. We both had a good income, we had pets and found the place we wanted to live in for at least a very long time, so buying a house seemed the logical next step. Within a week of seeing the house advertised, we had made an offer and had the offer accepted. We could not believe our luck. The half-a-million-dollar mortgage was a massive commitment, but we could pay it on one wage if we had to and finally we had a place we could make our own.

After we bought the house, my partner was content. I was not. What was the ultimate dream for him (and for many people in the Western world), turned out to be my worst nightmare. I never wanted to have a mortgage. I had never seen that for myself. I loved my partner so much, that I started believing that his dreams were my dreams. I lost myself in him and therefore, I lost track of who I truly was and what I wanted in life.

With the help of my psychologist and kinesiologist, I came back to what was truly important in my life. Personal growth and development, not the safety and security of having my own house and a steady job. What once was a relationship that helped me grow, now was a relationship I could not grow in any further.

I am forever grateful for the time I had with my ex-partner. He created the perfect conditions for me to feel stable and safe within myself. He helped me reconnect with nature and taught me to be more present. He helped me get to the place where I realised I needed to move on. He helped me get back to my true self and back on my path. It is because of him, that I had found myself again and learned so many lessons I otherwise would not have. I was able to grow more with him, than I could have ever done by myself.

5.1 Different levels of living

Abraham Maslow develop a theory in 1943 that many health professionals still use today. It is called the hierarchy of needs. The hierarchy or pyramid of consists of five levels of needs all humans have.

Maslow's levels of needs are:

1. Physiological: These are our basic human needs and include breathing, food, water, sex, accommodation.
2. Safety: Feeling safe and secure in our resources, such as housing, work, finances and health.
3. Love and belonging: A sense of belonging, friendships, intimate partner relationships.
4. Self-esteem: Confidence in yourself, respect to yourself and others.
5. Self-actualisation: Creativity, spontaneity, problem solving, acceptance of self, others and the world.

Maslow's theory is, that we cannot work on the next level if the needs of the first level are not fulfilled. For most of my life, I did not feel safe within myself. And even though my basic physiological needs were met, I could not work on the other levels until I had established a sense of safety. Being in a relationship with a man who made me feel safe, allowed me to keep working on myself.

Some of my clients have been homeless or were in an environment where they did not feel safe. Doing counselling and working on increasing your self-love and confidence, will not work until you have satisfied the needs of (stable) accommodation and safety. Maslow's hierarchy gives us a way of clearly seeing the steps to take to continue our personal growth and development.

I invite you to consider on what level of needs you are working on? Have you fulfilled your basic needs? Are you trying to work on something that is actually impossible in the circumstances you find yourself in?

5.2 Letting go of everything

Letting go of my partner was one of the hardest decisions I have made in my life. From the outside, there was nothing terribly wrong with our relationship. People warned me that the grass would not be greener on the other side of the fence. They projected their own fears onto me, making me doubt my decision. It took 6 months and trying everything I could think of to try and salvage our relationship. In the end, we both knew that we had chosen different paths and had to let each other go.

Grief is the most difficult emotional process I have experienced. Stages of shock, denial, anger, depression and acceptance came as a whirlwind into my life. One day I would be angry, another day I would be sad, another day I would not feel anything. But the pain was consistently there. I had experience grief before, when my family members passed away and when I migrated to Australia. But to let go of someone who you envisioned spending your whole life with, someone who was not only my partner but my best friend, was almost unbearable.

There were times I could do nothing but cry and lay curled up in the foetal position on the floor. Some days I would not leave the little studio I was now renting. Not only had I lost my relationship, I had lost my best friend, my home and half of my friends because of the break up. Luckily my Social Work knowledge helped me cope. I was able to recognise the losses and the stages of grief. I had the support of 2 therapists and some of my closest friends and my family, who were there for me every single day. I knew to express my grief through writing and making art.

The best medicine for grief is time. It takes time to process a loss, to heal that part of your heart that got ripped away. I learned to give myself time, to keep persevering on a path of selflove and expression until time would heal my wounds. And as most people had already told me, but what seemed impossible at the early stages of my newly single life, it took about a year for the worst to be over and before the pain started to ease.

The biggest lesson I learned from that year, was that we all experience losses in our life. And letting go is hard. When we think of grief, we often think of the grief after a loved one dies. But every time we lose something, whether a job, a home, a friendship, we experience the same grieving process in more or lesser degree.

The other thing I realised, is how often we humans hold on to things or people that no longer serve us. Because we get scared, often amplified by the fear of other people in your surroundings who feel you are not making the right choice. I was 32 and ready to 'throw away' everything I had worked for, and for what? To be single again? To having to try and find another partner, start from scratch? What if I do not find that person? What if I make the wrong choice?

My life was definitely not bad at all, so why would I risk it all? Because by holding onto something that did not make me truly happy and trying to conform with the choices that are glorified in our culture, I could not stay true to myself. And it is only a matter of time before it starts eating away at your soul.

I had to let go of everything, but most of all, I had to let go of the fear that was inside me. Fear of what the future would bring for the newly single, 'middle-aged' me. And, as it turned out, it was the best thing I had done for years. I had finally chosen to do what was best for me, not for my partner or the people around me, but for me alone. And when I decided to choose for me, allowed myself to feel and work through the pain that inevitably comes with loss, doors opened for me that had never been opened for me before.

Grief and loss and what to do with it

We all experience losses in our lives. It is inevitable. Whether it is a loved one dying, a relationship ending, a relocation, a child moving out of home. Some of us experience many losses in their life. Big losses that come with traumatic experiences. The worst loss being the loss of love for ourselves.

When we experience a big loss or multiple losses, we experience grief. The grieving process has a set of stages that almost all people seem to experience. Dr Elisabeth Kubler Ross developed a model to help people understand this process, called the five stages of grief.

The five stages of grief by Dr Kubler Ross are:

- Denial
  Shock, feeling like the loss did not happen
- Anger
  Feeling angry about the loss, blaming yourself, others or God / the universe
- Bargaining
  Asking what if? And why? Trying to find ways to prevent the loss from happening
- Depression
  Feeling low, numb, guilt, emotional, extremely sad
- Acceptance
  Even though it is painful, you accept the loss has happened and continue to move forward

The stages do not necessarily unfold from denial through to acceptance. Although most people start with the phase of denial, we tend to move in and out of different stages. There might be days where we are accepting of the loss we experience, where the next day we are back to feeling low and angry about it.

Different people experience different symptoms, but a lot of people recognise the different stages. Most people experience difficulty sleeping or sleeping too much, lack of eating, nausea, not wanting to socialise. Recognising that all these sensations are part of a process that everyone experiences, can make the pain of grief more tolerable.

Annelieke de Vries

Time appears to be the master healer when we experience loss. Time and self-care. Time to express our emotions, and to know that there will be a day when the grief becomes less painful. The day we find a place for that loss in our heart and move forward. Until that day, all we can do is be gentle and nurturing towards ourselves. To write about our feelings, to cry, to paint or dance them out. And to be okay with the days where you cannot leave the house, or even the bedroom. It is okay, just breathe. Put your hand on your heart and breathe. Remember that the feelings never last, that there will be a time you feel different, happy, again.

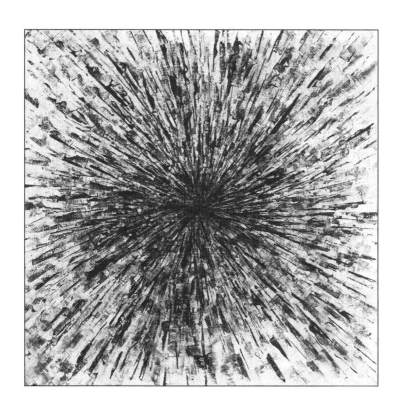

My grief on canvas

5.3 Mindfulness and meditation

I have attended many workshops about therapy models for my work, but one of them really made a difference in my personal life. It was one of those pivotal moments in my awakening and healing process. In 2012, I decided to travel to Brisbane for a workshop in Acceptance and Commitment Therapy by Dr Russ Harris. Two days of intense training in a new therapy model I had not heard of previously but was rapidly gaining momentum in the therapy world. As I always applied what I learned on myself, I actively participated in every exercise and critically reviewed the theory based on my own trauma and experiences.

I remember leaving the workshop in tears of relief. It was like a revelation. What I had learned was not only the importance and skills to be fully present with the things I did in my life (mindfulness), but the fact that everyone experiences bad or negative thoughts. That we cannot change the thoughts that come into our mind, only how we deal with them. I realised that I was not the only one who had suicidal or terrible thoughts which made me feel like a bad person. But the most pivotal moment was the realisation that there was more to me than my thoughts. That I was not my thoughts.

YOU ARE NOT YOUR THOUGHTS. THOUGHTS ARE JUST WORDS, LETTERS. YOU ARE THE ONE WHO GIVES THEM POWER BY BELIEVING THEM AS THE TRUTH.

What? My mind was blown. I had never seen myself separate from my thoughts. I learned that it was not about thoughts being positive or negative or true or false, only whether they were helpful to me (in the long-term) to live the life I wanted to live. I started seeing my brain in a different way, as a computer who tries to solve the problem of pain. It was my job to filter the solutions to see which would be the most helpful and effective in the long term, and to unhook from thoughts and solutions that were not.

To be able to see thoughts as nothing more than words, gave me my power back. I had never realised how much of my power I gave away to my thinking brain. I felt helpless to the thoughts I had, unable to let them go or even distance myself from them. I was my thoughts. To gain the knowledge and tools to separate myself from my thoughts was incredibly liberating.

The workshop also delved into emotions and value based living. I had always felt things so intensely, that the pain of sadness and depression and the panic of anxiety was often too much for me to bear. I would drown in emotion or disconnect from my feelings completely. Or I would resort to sex or drugs to numb the pain. Now I learned that if I would open to the feeling instead of avoiding it, breathe into it, make room for it and express it (expansion), it would not overwhelm me.

I looked into my values, the things that were most important to me: love, honesty, creativity, passion, happiness, adventure, compassion, connection. I looked at different aspects of my life and how close I was to living in line with my values. I was not. I had steered far away from my values, lost my creativity and passion in life and I certainly was not connected to myself or the world around me. It was harsh to be confronted with this, but it was the truth. By moving away from my values, I had moved away from my true self.

I started to do mindfulness meditations to learn to be more in my right brain, the observing self, the part that can watch all feelings and thoughts come and go. I struggled massively. My mind could not stay in the observing self, thoughts would constantly hook me in and take my attention away from the meditation. My mind objected left right and centre, telling me this was not for me, that I could never learn to do this properly. It was trying to confirm that age old story of 'there is something wrong with me'. But I persevered and tried to unhook from unhelpful thoughts whenever I noticed I got sucked in again.

The first few months of meditation were painful. I had high expectations of myself and when I would not do my meditations for a few days, I would beat myself up about it. But slowly mindfulness became easier and easier. I started practising it more in day to day life, even for a minute. To be more present when I ate my food or sat in session with a client, to really feel the sun and wind on my skin and see the different shades of green in the grass on my lunch break walk. I bought Russ Harris' book 'The Happiness trap', which became like a bible to me and many of my clients and friends.

The more I became mindful and practised defusion and expansion, the less the unhelpful thoughts came back. They will never go away completely, I was told that very clearly in the workshop. It is part of our evolution as a species to watch for danger and to think of the worst-case scenario. But I was no longer a victim to those thoughts. I could see them for what they really were: words, a picture, nothing more. And I could make the decision whether the danger was real, or a product of the trauma I had endured in my life. I learned to unhook from those thoughts, positive or negative, the ones that did not serve me. I started noticing my feelings more in my body and at times was able to name and express them and let them go without using avoidance techniques. I had taken my power back and slowly starting changing my story from 'There is something wrong with me', to 'I am a normal human being who feels pain'.

Mindfulness

Mindfulness is the art of being present. To quiet your mind and be completely present with the thing you are doing. We spend a lot of time caught up in our thoughts. So much so, that we forget to pay attention to what we are doing. We blank out in conversations or do not remember how we got from home to work. Mindfulness helps you strengthen the observing self. This is important, as this is the access to your soul, intuition or divine guidance.

The more we practise mindfulness, the more we are able to let thoughts come and go without getting caught up in them. The more we strengthen the observing self, the more we are able to connect with our soul. Mindfulness can be practised in many forms, including meditation. The good thing is that meditation is like bodybuilding, it helps the muscle in our brain strengthen rapidly.

I found it very difficult to get into a regular mediation routine. My thoughts and ego were too loud, telling me that it was a waste of my time. Instead of giving up, I changed my focus to practising mindfulness in daily life. I would walk around the block in my lunch break, focussing only on the sounds I could hear around me and the sun and wind I could feel on my skin. I started sitting down for my meals, focussing on really tasting the food instead of rushing like I would usually do. I would notice the sensations of the water in the shower. Outside I focussed on seeing the different shades of green in the hedges and grass. I started realising how much beauty I have been missing. How much I had not noticed before, in a place I had worked for two years already.

I slowly learned to let go of my thoughts that would come up every couple of seconds. This is normal, I found out at Dr Russ Harris' workshop. Even people highly trained at meditation, still get caught up in their thoughts at times. The aim of mindfulness is not to remove thoughts, but to allow them to come and go and learn to refocus your attention on the present moment. Practising mindfulness in my every day, strengthened my observing self enough to help me stay more present in my meditations.

5.4 Acceptance and Commitment Therapy

Acceptance and Commitment Therapy (ACT) is a therapy based on mindfulness, the skill of being present. It focusses on giving you new ways to manage your thoughts and feelings, and take action guided by your values. If you would like to know more about ACT, I encourage you to look up Dr Russ Harris' work. In this book, I will only touch on the parts of ACT that have made a significant difference for me in my journey.

Dr Russ Harris is the Acceptance and Commitment Therapy guru in Australia, and author of many self-help books based on this therapy. One of his books particularly helped me and many of my clients: The Happiness trap. It has been one of my bibles for many years, and I would highly recommend it to anyone. It includes many different ways of practising mindfulness and how to manage your thoughts and feelings that have helped me so much. Dr Russ Harris' informative website and YouTube channel are also worth visiting.

A different way to look at your thoughts

The biggest thing I got out of the first workshop with Dr Russ Harris, was that I realised that I was not my thoughts. That my thoughts are a part of me, but not the whole of me. He made me understand that everyone has bad thoughts, that this is part of how our brain has evolved. That this does not make me a bad person. That this does not mean that these thoughts are true or important.

I got a part of my power back after that workshop. Suddenly I realised that I was the one who gave my thoughts power over me. That thoughts are merely words. Letters that form words. Words that form sentences. Nothing more, nothing less. The more we focus on these words, the more we believe they are true, the more power we give them. It does not matter whether thoughts are true or false. In ACT, thoughts are not seen as good or bad, just as helpful or unhelpful. A few questions helped me separate the helpful from the unhelpful thoughts. Is this thought helping me to reach my goals? Is this thought serving my highest good? If it does not, I refocus my attention back on the present moment, remind myself it is normal to have these thoughts and let it go.

How do you look at your thoughts? Can you observe which thoughts are helpful for you to reach your goals, make your dreams become reality? Or are they holding you back in some way? How much power do you give to your thoughts? The aim is not to try and get rid of your thoughts, but to let them come and go, without getting hooked in to the unhelpful ones. Again, the more you practise this, the easier it gets.

Making room for your feelings

I have always struggled to connect with my feelings fully. As an empath, I feel everything so intensely. And when trauma happened, the emotions became too much. The ACT workshop taught me how to connect to my feelings, without losing myself in them. Instead of trying to fight a feeling, I learned to turn my attention towards it. To breathe into the feeling and make room for it. I learned to explore my feelings with curiosity. What is this feeling? Where does it start, where does it finish? Can I give it a colour? Is it hot or cold, fluid or sold, moving or still?

I learned to put my hand on my heart and label the emotion, reminding myself that it is natural to feel sadness, anger or fear. That it is a normal part of being human. That the feeling will subside again, like the waves of the ocean. All of this made the feeling less overwhelming. I learned to breathe into it and sit with it. I learned to recognise and release the emotions in my body through breathing, crying and art.

Looking at your values

Values are our soul's way of telling us what the best way is to behave in life. They are our moral compass, which helps us guide the actions we take. Everyone has different values, although some values are more common. Knowing what your values are, also helps us to recognise on which level we need to change in order to come closer to our values. The more our actions are in line with our values, the more we feel happy within ourselves.

I knew my values pretty well when I went to Dr Harris' workshop. What he made me realise though, was that I did not apply those values much to myself. I valued respect and connection and acted out of these values to others, but I was not very connected or respectful to myself.

There are many lists of values you can find online, but I will give you a few examples of common values:

- Love
- Health
- Family
- Connection
- Honesty
- Respect
- Creativity
- Forgiveness
- Caring

- Adventure
- Happiness
- Courage
- Humour
- Trust
- Loyalty
- Equality

I invite you to have a look at your values. Do you know what they are? How much are you acting in line with your values on all levels of your being? Are you applying them to yourself, as well as in connection to others?

6

The journey to self-love

After my relationship broke down, I did what many people do after they have been in a long-term relationship that has ended: drink and party my sorrows away. As I have mentioned before, I had a long history of numbing my feelings with drugs, alcohol and men. I started going out every week, dragging one of my closest friends with me to the pubs and nightclubs, until I went home to have sex with a man I met that night. Desperately seeking to make the pain more bearable and to have someone to depend upon. I am still very grateful for all the times my dear friend was there to help me ease the pain in the way I wanted to, without judgement.

The men I met were selfish, arrogant and even abusive. All I wanted was for someone to love me, so I could pick up the pieces of my broken self-esteem and feel good about myself. To ease the pain. It did not help. The drugs and alcohol helped temporarily, the sex sometimes would make me feel better for a brief moment. But mostly, I felt worse the next day than I had before I went out. And yet I continued in the same cycle, expecting a different outcome every time. Of course, the outcome did not change.

I continued this cycle for almost 6 months and could not seem to figure it out. Why did I attract men that treated me like shit, that made me feel inferior, that would leave quickly in the morning and would never text back? But after 6 months things did change. I started to attract more and a better quality of men into my life. What changed? I did. I started changing my story from 'I am not good enough' to 'any man is damned lucky to have me'. How? The answer is almost too simple: I started loving and respecting myself more.

The mindful self-compassion training I decided to do, and the continuous effort of daily meditations with self-compassion phrases started to pay off. Even though I did not believe in positive affirmations when I started, slowly they helped me change my story. I started accepting the whole of me and started loving myself for who I was. And I started to respect myself more, by setting boundaries and moving away from people and situations that did not serve me. I had heard of the law of attraction, but I always thought I had a pretty good self-esteem and so I should be able to attract the right people into my life. I had done work on myself to grow since I was seventeen and had built up a lot of confidence in my role as a sister, a daughter, a friend and a Social Worker. But when it came to men, I crumbled. I would give my power away instantly. I would become this small, insecure girl that just wanted to be loved, do the right thing and receive approval.

It was not until my internal story started to change, that I could change my behaviour. A male friend once told me that it is not how a girl looks that is attractive to him, but how confident she is within herself. My friend was right. The more my self-confidence grew and the more I started to accept, respect and love myself, the more I started attracting the same energy in men. As I am writing this book I am still single. Not because I cannot find a man to love me, but because there are times in our lives where we need to be alone to learn certain lessons in our life, and times where we can grow more with someone else than we can alone. It is up to us to constantly reflect where we are in our lives, and with whom we choose to connect with, or whom to let go off (even temporarily), to be able to continue to grow.

6.1 Mindful self-compassion

In 2016, I attended a 6-week intensive training in yet another therapy model, based on mindfulness: Mindful self-compassion (MSC). This was another pivotal moment in my recovery and awakening. I learned a skill

I needed desperately, as I was still very hard on myself and would often get hooked into the 'not good enough' story. I learned the skill of self-compassion and self-love.

Being kind to myself was a totally new concept for me. I was very good at being loving, compassionate and patient with my clients and friends, but not with myself. When I started practising MSC meditations regularly during the training, many emotions were brought up. I was overwhelmed with what is known as the grief of relief. I realised how hard I had been to myself all those years, how little I had been there for me. The grief was overwhelming. Luckily, I had some more tools to manage the feelings that came up and Marihuana was still a reliable friend to ease the pain as well.

For 24 years, since I lost connection to many part of myself in my childhood, I had beaten myself up and this made difficult feelings and unhelpful thoughts even more difficult. I had been my own dictator and biggest critic. I had never told myself I love me, that I am good enough with all my flaws and all my qualities. I had always relied upon others to tell me those things, and even then, my mind would object. It did not fit into the story I had about myself.

Even though I did not really believe in the self-compassion phrases (may I be safe, may I be happy) and my mind protested a lot, I persevered. Within a month, I started noticing a difference. I became being more kind to myself. I chose to do more nurturing supportive things for me, like taking the time to have a bath or spending that extra money to buy the salt lamp I had wanted for years. And it felt good.

What was harder to learn, was practising self-love through boundary setting and removing myself from things, situations and people that were not serving me. This is still the hardest part of self-compassion for me today. I was very good at helping other people and would always understand why people would react the way they did. Knowing their stories and their behaviour was only a product of trauma, it was easy to get lost into endless giving. Setting boundaries around this was difficult for me. I had to learn that there is a distinct difference between self-love and selfishness. That selfishness means to do things for you, no matter what the consequences are for others or the world we live in. And that self-love and self-compassion actually create more love and compassion for others and the planet. Through self-compassion, I learned I can help others better if I love and look after myself first. I finally started to understand phrases such as 'Help the world, start with yourself.'

Mindful Self-Compassion (MSC) explained

Mindful Self-Compassion is a therapy is based on developing self-compassion. This means developing love, forgiveness and acceptance of yourself, by practising mindfulness and reminding ourselves that all our thoughts and feelings are part of being a normal human being. Dr Christopher is one of the teachers of MSC and author of another one of my bibles: The mindful path to self-compassion.

I have grown up in a culture where I was taught that it is selfish to put yourself first. That we have to look after others first. Self-compassion does not mean you have to be selfish. Self-compassion is the ability to put yourself first, without disrespecting or affecting others in a negative way. To be able to give more to others by giving more to yourself. When we develop more compassion for ourselves, we automatically develop more compassion for others.

How to love yourself more

There are many ways to develop more self-love, but a few things have really helped me change my story about myself. One way I changed how I felt about myself, was to decide I deserved the best and start acting towards it. Even little things, like having a nice bath towel to dry myself with or lighting some candles helped a lot. My bath towel became a reminder of my self-love every time I had a shower. So did the salt lamp I finally bought for myself and the nice dress I decided to put on, even if I had no plans of going out. Every time I took the time to treat myself, do something nice for me, my self-love grew.

MSC works with self-compassion phrases, also known as positive affirmations. By meditation or at least saying these affirmations every day, I reconditioned my brain. My ego struggled a lot with the affirmations. May I be happy. "I am not happy!", my ego would scream. But as I let my ego scream and decided to do it anyway, I could start seeing the change within myself. It became easier to see my qualities and put myself first. The meditations that have helped me so much, are available for free to download on Dr Germer's website. I highly recommend you try them regularly for a month and see what happens!

6.3 Little parts of self and healing trauma

In 2017 I attended yet another training, this time a trauma workshop by one of the leading trauma experts Dr Janina Fisher. By this time, I realised I myself had experienced trauma and that most of my clients' mental health problems stemmed from traumatic life experiences. I understood that everyone experiences something traumatic at some stage in their life, in more or lesser degree. I read some books about trauma and trauma treatment, but still felt underqualified in this area.

In the workshop I was introduced to the Structural Disassociation Model, a model used to heal complex trauma. My mind was blown again. I left the workshop crying out of gratitude. I had finally found all the information I needed to heal my own trauma, and that of my clients.

I learned that, when trauma occurs, our personality splits into little parts of self that find ways to cope in a world that is perceived as unsafe. That we lose little parts of ourselves along the way, because they did not get what they needed at the time. I discovered the survival mechanisms these little parts of me had built up to protect myself. Everything started to fall into place. I finally understood where my dependency on men and drugs came from. Where my suicidal thoughts and disassociation were based in. And I learned more about the mind-body connection, that physical sensations and unhelpful thoughts and behaviours were communications from little parts of me, trying to tell me something and trying to keep me safe.

Little by little I got to know those parts of myself I had disconnected from. I could visualise my little 8-year-old self, who was so scared to be left alone and needed someone to depend upon. I noticed when she would raise her head, every time I felt a craving for male attention and physical intimacy. And I got to know my 15-year-old self, the one who would run to drugs, disordered eating or disassociation every time life got too overwhelming.

Slowly, I build a relationship with my little child-parts. I would notice them when certain thoughts or sensations would come up, and I would ask them two questions: What is it that you are worried about? What can I do to make you feel safer? The answers were often the same. The 15-year-old would tell me she is only protecting my little 8-year-old self. And that if I would take over, she would not have to resort to drugs or disassociation to protect her. The 8-year-old was clear in what she needed. She just needed me to be there for her and hold her. I would give to them what they needed. I would visualise holding my little 8-year-old self, like a mother holding her child. And I would tell her that she is safe now, that I am here for her now and apologise for all the times I had not been there in the past.

It was hard for my little child-parts to trust me at first. I quickly won the heart of my 8-year-old self, but my 15-year-old self was not that keen. It was not until I consistently started to give my little parts what they needed, that she started trusting me. In time, we went from hesitant 'high 5's' to group hugs. Every time I engaged with my child-parts and gave them what they need (and did not get in the past), I created a healing experience. Slowly I was resolving my childhood trauma and build up more effective ways of coping. More and more I was able to let go of unhelpful survival mechanisms, and resort to my strengths instead.

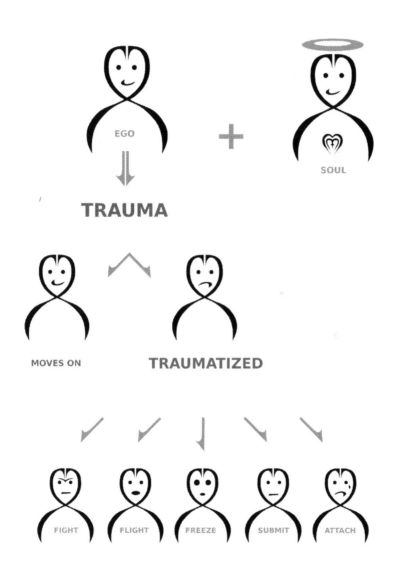

Parts of self

Parts of self

Dr Fishers' work helped me to get back in touch with the little parts of self I lost along the way due to trauma. What I took away from this workshop, is what I will share with you here. I refer to Janina Fishers book, Healing the fragmented self, for those who are interested in learning more about trauma and the Structural Disassociation Model (SDM).

When trauma happens, our personality splits. There is a part of you that will keep putting on a brave face. This is the part of you that keeps going on, no matter what, because we still have to go to work, raise our children, etc. The other part of the personality is traumatised. It is terrified and on high alert, waiting for the trauma to repeat itself. When even more trauma happens, the personality splits again. The part of you that keeps going on, might split into a different work, social and parent personality. The traumatised part, splits into five little parts. These parts are called: fight, flight, freeze, submit and attach. I believe that we all have these parts, as we all suffer from trauma in more or lesser degree due to the conditioning we endure in our lives.

I will briefly go over each part of self:

- Fight: this part is your angry part. It is the part that fights, and uses aggression, self-harm and suicidal thinking as ways of coping.
- Flight: this part that wants to escape. It wants to run, and uses addictive behaviour, disorder eating and ambivalence to cope.
- Freeze: this part is fearful, terrified. It uses freezing, panic attacks and social anxiety as coping mechanisms.
- Submit: this part of you feels shame. It I the part that has learned to submit, to be the good girl or boy. To take care of others, in order to keep yourself safe. Its symptoms are depression, self-hate and self-sacrifice.
- Attach: this is your needy part. It craves connection and wants to be rescued. It wants someone to depend upon, so it can feel safe. This part is innocent, naïve and sweet. It is the part that screams: help me!

There is also a part of us, that is not affected by trauma. This is the part of ourselves, that can give the other parts what they need. It is also known as the higher self, wise mind, or soul. In this model all sensations, thoughts and feelings inside ourselves, are seen as a communication of one of these parts. When we start noticing and recognising which sensations are telling us what part of ourselves wants attention, we can learn to connect with that part and give it what it needs. In this way, we can heal the trauma that made us lose the connection to those parts of self. This way, our soul or higher self provides the nurturing support needed, to develop good attachment within yourself. Your soul becomes the parent, giving you what you did not get at the time the trauma happened.

We need our parts of self. It is important to acknowledge and learn to accept all parts of us, even the ones we do not like very much. All parts are ways of coping that have kept you safe for many years. And they are still keeping you safe today. We have to be grateful to them for this. All our parts of self can be turned into strengths. When we connect to them and give them what they need, they become our ally instead of our enemy. We cannot connect with other people if we do not have a submit part. We cannot run away from actual danger if we do not have a flight part. How would we be able to stand up for ourselves, if our fight part was missing? We need our parts to keep us safe and connected to ourselves and other people.

Getting to know your child parts

Understanding and getting to know your little traumatised parts of self, is crucial to healing trauma. By going through this model, I started recognising the parts. Dr Fisher uses certain techniques, to further get to know your little parts of self, which I have found extremely helpful. The way I have learned to reconnect with my all parts of self, is through listening to my body. When a craving for drugs comes up, I know it is my fight part talking. When I feel like having sex, my little attach part is coming up. I started recognising what sensations, thoughts and feelings were communications of which part of me. I learned to recognise how old my parts were. Clear memories of my eight-year old self came up for my attach part. The year my trauma happened.

I encourage you to explore your little parts of self. How old are they? Can you see them in your mind's eye? Every time a little part of you is trying to communicate through the sensations in your body, take time to sit with them. Visualise that part of you that is talking to you. Get to know it and ask it what it is worried about. Your little part might tell you that he or she is scared or angry. Ask what it is that you can do, in order for this part to feel safer. They often just want to know that you are there for them. They might need a hug or some recognition for the work they have been doing to keep you safe. One of my clients sits in meditation every night. She invites all her little parts of self to come and she asks each and every one how they are and what they need. Then she gives it to them. I thought this was a beautiful way of building a strong relationship with all the parts of you.

6.4 Who am I?

In 2016, after a long struggle with Bipolar and Alzheimer's, my grandmother passed away peacefully. I flew over to The Netherlands for a month to be with her and help care for her in her last days. She did not die until a week after I got back to Australia (she always was a fighter), but that did not matter. What mattered for me, was that I was able to be there for her in those last days.

As I mentioned earlier my grandfather's death was extremely traumatic for me. Since he died I always felt a strong connection to my grandmother, and she to me. She was not an easy woman to get to know, but nonetheless I enjoyed spending time with her. When I moved to Australia, I would often send her postcards, pictures and phone her up every now and then. She was always delighted to her from me. When she died, I knew she would be together with my grandfather again. I was at peace with it, as she had battled with her mind for long enough. That trip back to The Netherlands, my time looking after her and supporting my family in their grieving process, was what brought closure to my trauma.

I had done so much work on myself in that year, and after my grandmother died, I really felt like I had healed my childhood trauma. But now I was left with a new problem. I did not know who I was anymore. I had let go of 'being the depression and anxiety' and all the traits that I thought were part of my personality, fitted into a typical response to trauma. I had let go of so much stuff, that I had lost my identity completely. I did not know who I was, now that I no longer identified with the diagnosis.

Anxiety started to come back. Insecurities and worrying thoughts came back up. What was part of my true identity and what was part of survival mechanisms I had built up because of trauma? I remember seeing my kinesiologist, asking her if we could please work on this. She gave me a simple task: ask your mother what you were like in the womb, as a baby and as a very young child, before all the conditioning of culture and trauma. My mother told me the pregnancy was easy, the birth effortless and quick. As a baby, I spewed a lot, but otherwise I was a happy, easy baby who sucked her thumb a lot. When I told my psychologist this, she was quick to point out that as a baby, I was able to self-soothe and regulate my emotions by sucking my thumb. The reflection of my psychologist helped me change that part of my story. From 'I need someone to help me not get overwhelmed by my emotions' to 'I am able to regulate my own emotions'.

As a young child, my mother remembered, I was always strong willed, wanting to do everything myself. I was also a child that was naturally very social and curious about people, caring and nurturing towards my little sister and all animals (I recall walking on my tippy toes so I would not hurt the ants), and even back then I loved the party scene, pointing out the lights and pubs in town and telling my parents "I want to go there". I did a brainstorm (word bubble) about myself. I put my name in the middle and through word association came up with all the words that fitted with me. I started looking into my family history and had a colleague do a proper Astrology reading for me.

About a year ago I decided to do a numerology report online. The 130 pages of information I received about myself were so recognisable, that it freaked me out a little. How is it possible that someone can tell me so much about myself, just from knowing my name and date of birth? My soul was too curious to not get tempted. I continued my research into numerology and researched my zodiac sign, my Chinese horoscope and my Mayan calendar.

All this research helped me piece the puzzle of who I was back together. It helped me distinct between my coping and my actual personality traits. It helped me rediscover my true self and change my story of who I was and am. And that was vitally important, because if I would have been left wondering, I know what would have happened. I would have gone back to what feels safe and what I knew. I would not have grown but would have reverted back to the old story I had about myself, and all the work I had done to change that story, would have been for nothing.

Finding your true self

There are many ways to rediscover who you truly are. I want to highlight a few tools that have helped me enormously in finding out who I truly was, and what my purpose is in this life.

Tools that can help to rediscover who you are:

- Numerology and Astrology reports. I recommend <u>www.numerologist.com</u> for a comprehensive online report.
- Look into your family tree and family history.
- Asking your parents or other family members about your personality traits as a young child.
- Brainstorming: put your name in the middle of a piece of paper, then start writing all the words that come up in your mind around your name. Focus on writing down everything you like about you.
- Write down all your passions, make a list of all the things you like about yourself (or what others like about you), and all the things that make you unique.
- Ask your friends or family to describe you in a few words.
- Have a look at your values.

7

How drugs changed my world

I have been interested in different drugs and the effects on the human brain since my teenage years. Working in mental health from a young age, I had seen the downside of drug use. Clients coming in with drug-induced psychosis made me well aware of the risks of drug-use. Besides using Marihuana and Alcohol, I was wary of it all. I did not know how it would affect my mental health. When I attended my first music festival at 15, I witnessed a girl in a bad trip first hand. All of this was enough to make me decide that I would not try psychedelics or hard drugs until I felt stable in my mental health.

When I was 17, I made a new group of friends who introduced me to the electronic music scene. A big group of us would go to big techno raves and drug use was plentiful among my friends. I tried MDMA for the first time and was hooked. I loved the feeling of love for everything and everyone, and the energy to fully immerse myself into my dancing. I never used much, enough to keep me going all night. I never mixed my drugs either, I knew what the effects could be. I started using it almost every weekend, it was my one night a week where I could let go of my Depression and Anxiety and dance it all out.

Little did I know back then, that what I was doing is called micro-dosing and that micro-dosing with MDMA has been proven to be a very effective treatment for trauma. It worked. Those nights filled with love were what kept me going. Marihuana would dull the pain during the week, MDMA would give me a break from suicidal thoughts and feelings of unworthiness and hopelessness.

After my grandmother passed away in 2016 and I felt I had healed most of my childhood trauma, I decided I was stable enough to give LSD a go. I met a man who was a highly experienced psychedelics user and who became a good friend. I trusted him and felt safe enough with him to allow him to guide me through my first trip. We went camping in the bush for a night and took half a drop of liquid LSD. It was like doing ten years of therapy in one night. My whole world fell apart in that first trip. I got to experience the concept that I rationally knew, but never had felt. That we are all one, that all living beings are connected, made out of the same energy. There was no separation between me and my friend, or me and the trees. I had never felt that much love for myself, never felt that connected to my body. And unlike MDMA or alcohol, I was more aware of my boundaries and safety. What was good for me and what was not had never been so clear. For the first time in my life, I experienced a full separation from my ego. I could notice thoughts and feelings and urges come up, but where normally there would be an instant behavioural response, on LSD I had the opportunity to pause and reflect before acting on that impulse.

I was reflecting on everything during the trip, to see what was different in this altered state of consciousness. What was different in my thinking? How did I feel about my body now? How did I feel about smoking and different foods? Did it change my perspective on others and the world around me and how and why? How did I feel about my work, trauma and the therapy models I used? It was what I call a positive traumatic experience. It was like I had finally woken up and could see myself, others and the world around me for what they really were. I remember crying in the car driving back to town the next day. Tears of gratitude for all the beauty in this world. That one trip turned my world upside down. It changed me dramatically, for the better.

7.1 Psychedelics as a tool to grow

I knew that integration of this experience was vital. I wanted to process this positive trauma properly and achieve the changes in my behaviour and thinking in my day to day life, without the use of psychedelics. I spend two weeks writing, reflecting and doing art about my LSD trip. I made conscious choices to brave my anxiety (that obviously came back after the trip), to ensure I would integrate what I had learned. Writing my diary helped me recall memories of that very important 24 hours in my life. The more I wrote, the more details of the trip came back into my conscious mind. Painting and writing and talking about what happened, helped me reflect on my fears and see clearly what I needed to let go of them. It was not until after the trip and the high of what I had experienced subsided a bit, that the hard work started.

One of the choices I made was to purposely not wear bras anymore. During the trip was the first time in my life where I was fully connected to my body. The first time I could accept my looks and see my beauty. I have small breasts, which had been a continuous point of insecurity for me. I wore push-up bras to make them look bigger. No more. I decided I was okay with my body, I did not need to change my appearance anymore. I remember the first week clearly. I was anxious when I would walk out of my front door to face other people, bra-less. But I persevered and the new behaviour replaced the old. I felt more confident and more comfortable with my body every time I made that conscious choice. And this help me further connect to myself.

Psychedelics are not wonder drugs that solves everything. I can see how people can use it for fun and not learn anything, instead fleeing into a world that is much prettier and filled with love as just another way of coping. But for me, it was exactly what I needed. I rationally knew that we are all connected and that there is no time and space as we know it. But to actually be in a complete state of mindfulness, to feel the connection to the earth and all living beings, to feel the state of love for myself I had never felt before. That is something different. To not operate from a place of ego and fear, but from soul and mindfulness, it really cemented all I knew rationally into my whole being. I finally felt what it was like, to be my true self and to see the world the way it truly was.

Everything has a purpose

I can see the power of LSD and other psychedelics. I have experienced its therapeutic benefits within myself so clearly. The world is slowly catching up and the therapeutic benefits of psychedelics are finally being researched again. One of the big things I learned from using psychedelics and plant medicine, is that nothing is good or bad. Everything in this world has a purpose. It is the way we use it that can be named good or bad. Plants such as tobacco, Marihuana, DMT, Magic Mushrooms and San Pedro all have their purpose. Just like money and technology have a purpose. All can be used for good and for bad. I learned that tobacco can help cleanse you from lower vibrations. I started to understand that Marihuana and San Pedro are teachers, helping me to come back to my soul, reflect upon my ways, and let go of what does not serve my highest good.

Understanding the purpose of everything in life helped me understand myself better. I could see how Marihuana has been a teacher for me for a long time, and it gave me more understanding as to why I smoke. I started reflecting upon when I would smoke tobacco, and realised it was whenever I felt I had picked up low vibrations from other people. It helped me cleanse my aura and helped to ground me. This in turn helped me be more acceptant of myself and helped me start using substances more purposefully.

7.2 Tips for safe trips

Psychedelics, including magic mushrooms and LSD, are not for everyone. I am not trying to promote drug use, but merely provide safe guidelines on how to use it, if you are going to do it anyway. The therapeutic benefits of psychedelics are coming back into the public eye and when used appropriately they can be a valuable healing tool. If it does not feel right for you, it is not right. Never go against your feelings, trust your intuition and only use these drugs (or medicines) when you feel you are ready. Remember, psychedelics are still illegal in most countries in the world. Some tips for safe trips:

- Do not take psychedelics if you don't feel ready!
- Never mix your drugs with other drugs or alcohol.
- Make sure you have a reliable supplier that provides a good quality product. I never use anything that has not been tried by one of my friends already. You can buy test kits online to test the purity at home.
- Have a good meal beforehand, you might not want to eat during the trip.
- Use psychedelics with the respect they deserve. They are extremely powerful tools that can send you mad if not used safely and with respect. I have a ritual that I do before any trip, where I set my intentions (what I want to get out of this experience) and show my respect to the energies I work with.
- Set and setting is everything when using psychedelics. Be in a place where you feel safe. Do it with other people who you trust and who are experienced users, especially the first few trips. Preferably be with someone who is sober and can intervene or get help if anything happens.
- Research the psychedelic drug before use, so you know a bit about the effects and how long the trip will take. In my experiences, mushroom trips seem to last about 6 hours (of which the first two very intense), LSD about 12-16 hours. A Dutch group of young adults have started a great YouTube channel called 'Drug Lab', where they test out different drugs on camera and show more tips for safe use. The Multidisciplinary Association for Psychedelic Studies (MAPS) is another great resource. Their website includes information and guidelines for therapeutic use for different psychedelic drugs.
- Drink plenty of water and have food handy for when you get hungry. It is easy to lose track of time and become dehydrated. You are using an intense amount of energy tripping, so make sure you drink enough.
- Ensure that you have plenty of time after a trip to rest, refuel and integrate. Write, draw, dance and talk about your experience. Write as much down as you remember, to help memory recall, release emotions generated by the trip and help process the experience.

A Final Word

After 33 years of being on a pursuit of happiness, I can finally say that I no longer am. I have found the peace and happiness I have been looking for, in every moment in every day. I no longer give my power away to anyone or anything. I remember my true self, accept myself with all my flaws and all my qualities and know my purpose in this life. I can say, with confidence, that I have mastered being human. Most of the time.

I mean, I am still human and this design inevitably comes with flaws. I still get lost, experience pain and do things wrong. It comes with the human experience. Living in a world build on systems of fear, injustice and unfairness and in a human body that is conditioned with trauma for generations, it is only natural to get off track and lose ourselves at times. But I no longer resist the pain, and therefore I no longer suffer. I no longer depend on anything or anyone for my happiness and peace and internal safety and stability. And when I do get lost, it does not take me long to find myself again and to pull myself back on the path of self-love.

I am not perfect or better than anyone else. I have so much more to learn. Learning and growing is part of life, and as long as I continue to live, I am dedicated to keep working on myself. So that I can be a better version of myself every day I wake up, and therefore a better friend, a better sister, a better daughter and a better counsellor.

Accepting the darkness to find the light

The first thing that goes through my mind when I get new information that helps me to grow, is: why? Why did I not know all of this 20 years ago? My life would have been so much easier. If I had remembered my true self and my purpose in this life, I would not have plunged deep into Depression and Anxiety. I would not have self-harmed or ended up in the cycle of addiction. I would not have experienced struggle and suffering. I would not have gotten lost.

Today I am grateful for every single experience I have had in my life, no matter how painful, no matter how lost I got. It has made me into the person that I am today. How would I have been able to understand or help my clients, if I had never experienced the dark side of life? How can I understand the value of joy, love, fun and play without experiencing depression, fear and anger? I needed to get lost, in order to find myself again.

My journey has made me come to a place of understanding that it is a gift to experience life on this earth. That it is a gift to experience both positive and negative. I have learned to not only accept, but to embrace duality. And only from this place, from my path through the darkness into the light, have I been able to realise that duality only exists in this physical world and not inside of us. Only because of my journey, have I been able to see that all I was made to belief about myself and my inner world is a lie. That duality is an illusion, promoted to keep you in a place of fear where you do as you are told. That we are only made of positive energy, love and light, the highest vibration. All that fear, sadness, anger and individuality are only results of generations of conditioning of living in fear. None of it was ever a part of us, but only became a part of us because we did not know how to acknowledge, accept and let it go.

There is only one choice

My world has become much simpler these days. There is only one choice to make, every moment of every day: do I choose love or fear? Do I choose to love, forgive and accept myself and focus on the beauty in the present moment, or do I allow myself to get caught up in worrying and fighting my feelings? Do I choose to brave my fears, or let my fears rule my world?

76

Self-love, forgiveness and acceptance is the key to a life filled with happiness, ease, beauty and purpose. The more we love and nurture ourselves, the more we get to know and accept all the part of us, the more we connect to ourselves. And it is this connection that leads to the connection with your soul and the universe or God. The more we focus on doing what fills our heart with joy, instead of what is expected of us, the more things start to flow in your life. Life becomes easier. The voice of your soul gets stronger, guiding you every step of the way. Work, friends, money will start flowing into your life, because you honestly know you deserve it.

Ask yourself the question every single day. Am I acting from a place of self-love or fear? Am I choosing to do things that are nurturing my soul, or eating away at it? Start noticing the patterns, observe when fear comes up and chose to brave your fears. Remember that only love is real. There is only fear of fear, and when you brave that darkness, you realise there is nothing but light on the other side. Pain is inevitable in this life, but suffering is not. It is a choice most of us never realised we had. Nothing can harm you unless you allow it to. You are the creator of your own reality. You can manifest your wildest dreams on earth. Brave your fears, and step into the realm of love and possibilities.

Word list

- Altered state of consciousness: Any state of being where we operate outside of our ego and thinking self. Altered states of consciousness can include: disassociation, being intoxicated out of body experiences, trance, meditation, lucid dreaming.
- Anxiety: feeling constantly stressed, worried or scared, having an overreaction to specific triggers (food, being around other people, spiders, etc).
- Awakening: no longer living in a place of fear, coming back to your true self, reconnection to self and therefore to others, the world around you and the power that connects us all.
- Coping-mechanism: a way of handling a situation, a way you have survived and kept yourself safe so far.
- Conditioning: training or programming of the brain through therapy, parenting, culture, media, etc.
- Counselling: cognitive therapy, psychological treatment.
- Depression: feeling low, unmotivated, hopelessness, no energy, can include suicidal thoughts.
- Disassociation: state of disconnection from self, feeling out of your body, unable to feel anything.
- Ego: our personality, sense of self, beliefs about yourself, others and the world we live in.
- Expressive arts: dance, visual art, poetry, writing, drama, body work, making music.
- Hyperarousal: state of fight/flight.
- Hypo-arousal: state of freeze, disconnection from self, disassociation.
- Meditation: A way of training the right brain and our observing self.
- Mindfulness: being fully present in the moment, with a focus on strengthening our observing self. It is a state of awareness and present, observing what is happening in and outside of yourself.
- Psychedelics: hallucinogenic drugs, such as MDMA and LSD, but also includes plant medicine such as San Pedro, Marihuana and Ayahuasca.

- Religion: a system that believes in a specific truth and has put in place rules to follow, in order to be accepted into this system.
- Self-love: be kind, loving, nurturing, forgiving and accepting of yourself as you are right now by doing things that make you feel happy and are good for your wellbeing.
- Self-care: the things you require in order to look after yourself, such as taking time to rest, eating health, having massages, etc.
- Self-compassion: showing respect, love, forgiveness and acceptance towards yourself.
- Spirituality: connection to self, others and the world around you and therefore with the universal consciousness.
- Stress response: fight/flight/freeze response.
- Soul: our higher self, our heart, divine guidance, intuition,
- Trauma: traumatic event that causes injury and change on all levels of our being.
- Trigger: something that reminds you consciously or subconsciously of past trauma and sets of a response in your mind and body.
- Universal consciousness: god, the divine, universal energy, lifeforce energy, higher power, the energy that connects all beings on this planet.
- Values: how you want to act as a human being, guidelines.

References

Books

Blink: the power of thinking without thinking, Malcolm Gladwell, 2005

The happiness trap, Dr Russ Harris, 2013

The mindful path to self-compassion, Christopher K Germer, 2009

Healing the fragmented selves of trauma survivors, Janina Fisher, 2017

A theory of human motivation, Dr Maslow, 1943

On death and dying, Dr Elisabeth Kubler -Ross, 1969

Websites

www.maps.org

www.christophergermer.com

www.janinafisher.com

www.actmindfully.com

Printed in the United States
By Bookmasters